STA

Edited by Denis Stevenson

sapling

First published in the U.K. in 1996 by Sapling,
an imprint of Boxtree Ltd, Broadwall House 21
Broadwall, London, SE1 9PL.

Printed in Great Britain by Cox & Wyman Ltd,
Reading, Berkshire
Typeset by SX Composing DTP

ISBN 0 7522 0247 2
A CIP catalogue entry for this book is available
from the British Library.

Like a phoenix, StarFiles rises from the ashes of Miller's Fanclubs. The first edition of Miller's Fanclubs proved so successful that the publication became an annual event. It was later produced as a diary by Collins, and a card collection. Fan clubs regularly come under scrutiny which is particularly pleasing as they are an integral part of the pop business, equally important to both the artist and fan. 'A healthy fan club means a continuously successful artist' is a maxim a number of stars could well adopt. There are far too many stars that are here today, gone tomorrow, and not all because they were lacking in talent. Fans will always want that special contact, the personal communication, which a well-run fan club provides. Fans like to associate with their idols, to belong. Fan clubs can and do satisfy that need.

We have purposely omitted subscription details in this edition because we feel that it is advisable to make contact in the first instance.

On receiving a reply, if you are satisfied with the package, only then forward the required subscription. Whenever writing we stress the importance of enclosing a stamped addressed envelope.

We have done our utmost to ensure the information in StarFiles is as accurate as possible at the time of going to press, but it has to be remembered that the time between research and publication is at least six months and changes are happening all the time. We are afraid that is still a characteristic of the pop business.

The complete support and enthusiasm of all the record companies and fan clubs has continued to an ever-increasing degree – a clear endorsement of their approval of the publication. Their cooperation and willingness to make available material has again proved invaluable. We hope you enjoy this edition of *Fanclubs* as much as we enjoyed compiling it and that it will once again provide you with the opportunity to enjoy that special personal contact with the stars you admire most.

Denis Stevenson.

We would like to thank all the record companies and individual fan clubs for their support and enthusiasm.

A&M Press Office
Arista Press Office
BMG
Chrysalis Press Office
Columbia Press Office
EMI Press Office
Epic Press Office
Island Records Press Office
Jive Records
London Records Press Office
MCA Press Office
Polydor Press Office
RCA Press Office
SONY
Virgin Records Press Office
WEA Press Office
Zomba Records

Special thanks to the Take That management and Todd Slaughter of the Elvis Presley fan club. Their cooperation, provision of material and permission to reproduce the many superb photos have all proved invaluable.

Acknowledgements

Contents

A

Aaliyah
c/o Zomba Records
165–167 High Road
Willesden
London NW10 2SG

Abba Around the World
Speelman Straat 16 III
1063ZH
Amsterdam
Holland

Absolutely Fabulous
c/o BBC TV Centre
Wood Lane
London W12 8QT
England

Ace of Base
c/o London Records
Chancellors House
Chancellors Road
Hammersmith
London W6 9SG

Aerosmith
PO Box 1443
Poole
Dorset
BN15 3YP
also
c/o Sony-Columbia
10 Great Marlborough
Street
London W1V 2LP

Andre Agassi
c/o International
Management
Group One
Erie View Plaza
Suite 1300
Cleveland
Ohio 844144
USA

AKA
c/o RCA
Bedford House
69-79 Fulham High
Street
London SW6 3JW

The Alarm
47 Bernard Street
St Albans
Herts
AL3 5QL

Mark Almond
Gutterhearts
166 New Cavendish
Street
London W1

The Almighty
c/o Rone Walters
The Almighty Info
Services
PO Box 022
Strathaven
ML10 6EW

Pamela Anderson
Baywatch
c/o LBS
Communications
875 Third Avenue
New York
NY 10022
USA

Amber
c/o Island Records
22 St Peters Square
London W6 9NW

Ant Banks
c/o Zomba Records
165-167 High Road
Willesden
London NW10 2SG

Apache Indian
c/o Island Records
22 St Peters Square
London W6 9NW

Tina Arena
c/o Sony-Columbia
10 Great Marlborough
Street
London W1V 2LP

Armoured Saint
PO Box 295
Temple City
California 91780
USA

The Assembly
PO Box 77
Walton-on-Thames
Surrey
KT12 5BN

Rick Astley
PO Box 50
Manchester
M15 4GY

Aswad Posse
c/o Island Records
22 St Peters Square
London W6 9NW

A Tribe Called Quest
c/o Zomba Records
165-167 High Road
Willesden
London NW10 2SG

B

Baama Maai
c/o Island Records
22 St Peters Square
London W6 9NW

Baby Face
c/o Epic Records
10 Great Marlborough
Street
London W1V 2LP

Bahia Black
c/o Island Records
22 St Peters Square
London W6 9NW

The Bangles
Bangles and Mash
4455 Torrance Blvd
Torrance
California 90503
USA

Basia
c/o Epic Records
10 Great Marlborough
Street
London W1V 2LP

Bawl
c/o A&M Records
136–144 New Kings
Road
London SW6 4LZ

**Beach Boys Freaks
United**
PO Box 8422 82
Los Angeles
California 90073
USA

Beach Boys Stomp
22 Avondale Road
Wealdstone
Middlesex
HA3 7RE

Jennifer Beals
132 South Rodeo Drive
Suite 110
Beverley Hills
California 90212
USA

Beatles
Info Only
Cavern Mecca
18 Matthew Street
Liverpool
L2 6RE
also
Beatles Unlimited
PO Box 602
3430 APN Ieuwegein
Holland

The Beautiful South
The Groove-a-Thon
PO Box 87
Hull
HU5 2EQ

Pat Benatar
890 Tennessee Street
San Francisco
California 94107
USA

The Big Breakfast
2 Lock Keepers
Cottages
Old Ford Lock
London E3 2NN

Bjork
PO Box 4219
London SW17 7XF

Blur
c/o Parlaphone Records
120 Manchester Square
London W1A 1ES

Marc Bolan
PO Box 10
Bath
Avon
BA1 1YH

Michael Bolton
c/o Sony-Columbia
10 Great Marlborough
Street
London W1V 2LP

Bon Jovi
Back Stage with Bon
Jovi
PO Box 326
Fords
New Jersey 08863
USA

**Bon Jovi Secret
Society**
PO Box 4843
San Francisco
California 94101
USA

Boyzone
PO Box 102
Stanmore
Middlesex
HA7 2PY

Elkie Brooks
c/o Lorraine Osbourne
Mapleleaf
Stapleford Road
Stapleford Abbots
Romford
Essex
RM4 1EJ

Brookside
Campus Manor
Abbey Road
Chidwell
Liverpool
L16 0JP
England

Bobby Brown
PO Box 1873/287
Encino
Los Angeles
California 91436
USA

Kate Bush
PO Box 120
Welling
Kent
KA16 3DS

11

C

Jim Carey
c/o New Life
116 North Robertson
Blvd
200 Los Angeles
California 90042
USA

Maria Carey
PO Box 679
Brandford
Connecticut 06405
also
c/o Sony-Columbia
10 Great Marlborough
Street
London W1V 2LP

Dina Carroll
c/o A&M Records
136-144 New Kings
Road
London SW6 4LZ

Carpenters
PO Box 1084
Downey
California 90028
USA

Carter
USM Clubcarter
PO Box 709
London SE19 1JX

David Cassidy
The Old Post House
The Street
Litlington
Polegate
East Sussex
BN26 5RD

Cher
5807 Homett Drive
Orlando
Florida 32808
USA

Christians
PO Box 45
Liverpool
L9 2LE

Linford Christie
The LCJ Club
PO Box 195
Richmond
Surrey
TW9 2UB

Eric Clapton
Slowhand
PO Box 1062
London NW1 5HP

Phil Collins
PO Box 107
London N65
England
also
Phil Collins News
PO Box 253
Princeton Junction
New Jersey 68550
USA

Alice Cooper
c/o Epic Records
10 Great Marlborough
Street
London W1V 2LP

Coronation Street
c/o Granada TV
Manchester
M60 9EA

Elvis Costello
28 The Butts
Brentford
England

The Cranberries
International Fan Club
PO Box 2660
Brighton
BN1 1SX

Beverley Craven
c/o Epic Records
10 Great Marlborough
Street
London W1V 2LP

Tom Cruise
c/o PMK
955 Carillo Drive
200 Los Angeles
California 90048
USA

Cud
c/o A&M Records
136-144 New Kings
Road
London SW6 4LZ

Culture Beat
c/o Epic Records
10 Great Marlborough
Street
London W1V 2LP

D

Terence Trent D'Arby
The Hardline Society
PO Box 910
London NW1 9AQ

Dead or Alive
PO Box 65
Liverpool
L69 6LG

Chris de Burgh
PO Box 276
London E2 7BW
also
c/o A&M Records

136-144 New Kings
Road
London SW6 4LZ

Jack Dee
The Curb
The Old Bakery
6a Philip Walk
London SE15 3NH

Deep Purple
Appreciation Society
PO Box 254
Sheffield
S6 5FL

Dennis the Menace
PO Box 66
Dundee
DD1 9LN
Scotland

Del Amitri
c/o A&M Records
136-144 New Kings
Road
London SW6 4LZ

Desperate Dan
PO Box 66
Dundee
DD1 9LN
Scotland

Deuce
c/o London Records
Chancellors House
72 Chancellors Road
Hammersmith
London W6 9SG

Celine Dion
PO Box 65
Repentigny
Quebec
J6A 5HY
Canada
also
c/o Epic Records

10 Great Marlborough
Street
London W1V 2LP
England

Dire Straits
Damage Management
10 Southwick Mews
London W2

Bob Dylan
Wanted Man
PO Box 18
Bury
Lancashire
BL9 0LX

Doctor Who
Appreciation Society
12 Steerforth Street
Earls Court
London SW18
also
Management Three
4th Floor
9744 Wilshire Blvd
Beverley Hills
California 90212
USA

E

East 17
Talking Heads
PO Box 153
Stanmore
Middlesex
HA7 2HF
England
also
c/o London Records
Chancellors House
72 Chancellors Road
Hammersmith
London W6 9SG
England

Eastenders
c/o BBC Elstree Centre
Clarendon Road
Borehamwood
Herts
WD6 1JE
England

Sheena Easton
c/o Harriet Wasserman
Management
3575 Cahuenga Blvd
West
Suite 470
Los Angeles
California 90068
USA

Eight Storey Window
c/o A&M Records
136-144 New Kings
Road
London SW6 4LZ

David Essex
Zibeon House
43 Wolverton Road
Boscombe
Bournemouth

Gloria Estefan
c/o Epic Records
10 Marlborough Street
London W1V 2LP

Eternal
Freepost
PO Box 460
High Wycombe
Bucks
HP12 4BR

Chris Evans
c/o BBC Radio One
London W1A 4WW

F

Dan Falzon
PO Box 1722
Livingstone
West Lothian
DH54 6XT
Scotland

Frear Power
Trinity Street
Freepost
47 Bedford Street
Leamington Spa
Warwickshire
CV32 5DY

Fresh No More
c/o London Records
Chancellors House
72 Chancellors Road
Hammersmith
London W6 9SG

Fresh Prince of Belair
DJ Jazzy, Jeff and Fresh
Prince
PO Box 1255
South Hampton
Pennsylvania 18966
USA

Frontier Worlds
2 Broadoaks Road
Sale
Cheshire
M33 1SR

Fry & Laurie
c/o Noel Gay Agency
19 Denmark Street
London WC2H 8NA

G

Michelle Gayle
c/o RCA Records
Bedford House
69-79 Fulham High
Street
London SW6 3JQ

Genesis
Info Only
PO Box 253
Princeton Junction
New Jersey 08550
USA

Gary Glitter
37 Blacksmith Lane
Rainham
Essex
RM13 7AD

Ryan Giggs
c/o MUFC
Old Trafford
Manchester
M16 0RA

Mel Gibson
c/o ICM
8899 Beverly Boulevard
Los Angeles
California 90045
USA

Gompic
c/o Epic Records
10 Great Marlborough
Street
London W1V 2LP

Greenday
c/o Wea Records
28 Kensington Church
Street
London W8 4EP

Gun
c/o A&M Records
136–144 New Kings
Road
London SW6 4LZ

Guns 'N' Roses
Conspiracies Inc
PO Box 67279
Los Angeles
California 90067
USA

H

Daryl Hall
c/o Epic Records
10 Great Marlborough
Street
London W1V 2LP

Tom Hanks
c/o Wm Morris Agency
151 Camino Drive
Beverley Hills
California 09212
USA

Lenny Henry
c/o PBJ Management
5 Soho Square
London W1V 5DT

Nick Heyward
c/o Epic Records
10 Great Marlborough
Street
London W1V 2LP

Jane Horrocks
7 Pinewood Grove
Huntingdon
York
YO3 9DF

Home and Away
The UK Official Fan Club
PO Box 525
Maidenhead
Berkshire
SL6 1YU

Whitney Houston
PO Box 1644
Englewood Cliffs

New Jersey 6732
USA

Human League
c/o Smerch
PO Box 1AP
London W1

I

Icet
Syndicate Fanclub
1283 La Brea Avenue
PO Box 211
Los Angeles
California 90019
USA

Billy Idol
c/o Jane Cheese
42 The Fairway
Brickley
Kent
BR1 2JY

INXS
Info Service
PO Box 107
London N6 5RU

Iron Maiden
PO Box 10
London SW19 3YW

J

Janet Jackson
14755 Ventura Blvd
No 1-710 Shelman
Oaks
California 914403
USA

Michael Jackson
5443 Beethoven Street
Los Angeles
California 90066
USA

also
c/o Epic Records
10 Great Marlborough
Street
London W1V 2LP

Jamiroquai
c/o Longlost Brothers
Unit 220
Camalot Production
Studios
222 Kensal Road
London W10

Joan Jett
PO Box 77505
San Francisco
California 94107
USA

Jett Lag
155 East 55th Street
Suite 64
New York
NY 10022,USA

Billy Joel
c/o Sony-Columbia
10 Great Marlborough
Street
London W1V 2LP

Elton John
EJ Fanclub
32 Galena Road
London W6

Howard Jones
102 Green Street
High Wycombe
Bucks

Tom Jones
c/o Sylvia Firth
205 Luck Lane
Paddock
Huddersfield
West Yorkshire
HD1 4RB

Joy Division
c/o London Records
Chancellors House
72 Chancellors Road
Hammersmith
London W6 9SG

K

R Kelly
c/o Zomba Records
165–167 High Road
Willesden
London NW10 2SG

Nicole Kidman
c/o Nancy Seltzer
6220 Dell Vale Drive
Los Angeles
California 90048
USA

King
Unity Club
PO Box 686
London SE19 2TH

Kiss
The Kiss Army
PO Box 840
Westbury
NY 11590
USA

Kriss Kross
c/o Sony-Columbia
10 Great Marlborough
Street
London W1V 2LP

L

Cyndi Lauper
c/o Epic Records
10 Great Marlborough
Street
London W1V 2LP

The Lemonheads
c/o Eastwest Records
46 Kensington Court
London W8 5DP

Annie Lennox
Unit 32
Ransomes Dock
35–37 Park Gate Road
London SW11 4NP

Lisa L'Anson
c/o BBC Radio One
London W1A 4WW

Let Loose
The Asylum
PO Box 46
Ashford
Kent
TN24 8YT

CJ Lewis
3 Alveston Place
Leamington Spa
Warwickshire
CV32 4SN

**Huey Lewis and
the News**
PO Box 888
Mill Valley
California 94942
USA

Gary Lineker
19 Charnwood Avenue
West One
Northants
NN3 3DX

Louise
PO Box 888
High Wycombe
Bucks
HP11 2NY

M

Paul McCartney
PO Box 4 UP
London W1A 4UP

Bittey McClean
c/o Victoria Williamson
76 Stanley Gardens
London W3 7BL

Kirsty McColl
128 Wellesy Road
Clacton-on-Sea
Essex
CO15 3PT

Madonna
8491 Sunset Blvd
485 West Hollywood
California 90069
USA

**Manic Street
Preachers**
c/o Epic Records
10 Great Marlborough
Street
London W1V 2LP

Barry Manilow
PO Box 40
Epsom
Ewell
Surrey
KT1 9EF

Sean Maguire
PO Box 650
Brighton
BN1 1TB

Menswear
Info Service
PO Box 628
Harrow
Middlesex
HA3 9BF

The Good Mixer
Public House
Inverness Street
Camden
London NW1

Meatloaf
PO Box 68
Stockport
Cheshire
SK3 0JY
also
c/o Epic Records
10 Great Marlborough
Street
London W1V 2LP

Kylie Minogue
PO Box 292
Watford
WD2 4ND
also
c/o Deconstruction
Records
Bedford House
67–79 Fulham High
Street
London SW6 3JW

MN8
CV744
Freepost
3 Alverston Place
Leamington Spa
Warwickshire
CV32 4BC

Moist
Moist Fanclub
c/o Chrysalis Records
EMI House
43 Brook Green
London W6 7EF

M People
c/o Deconstruction
Records
Bedford House
67–79 Fulham High
Street
London SW6 3JW

Monkees
Monkees HQ
6 Pinfolds
Warwick Court
Teviott Avenue
Aveley
Essex
RM15 4QA

Monkey Business
Fanzine
2770 South Broad
Street
Trenton
New Jersey 08610
USA

**The Monkee Manias
Club**
PO Box 9
Forest Hill
Victoria 3131
Australia

Demi Moore
c/o Columbia Pictures
10202 West
Washington
Culver City
USA

Morrissey
c/o RCA
Bedford House
69–79 Fulham High
Street
London SW6 3JW

Alison Moyet
Info Service
PO Box 5
Basildon
Essex
SS16 4ED
also
c/o Sony-Columbia

19

10 Great Marlborough
Street
London W1V 2LP

N

Naughty By Nature
PO Box 786
East Orange
New Jersey 07017
USA

Neighbours
PO Box 136
Walford
WD 4ND
England

Nirvana
PO Box 5239
Hoboken
New Jersey 07030
USA

O

Oasis
Trinity Street
Freepost
CV744
3 Alveston Place
Leamington Spa
CV32 4BA
Warwickshire

Billy Ocean
c/o Zomba Records
165–167 High Road
Willesden
London NW10 2SG
England

Chris O'Donnell
1875 Centry Park East
Suite 1300
Los Angeles
California 90067
USA

Sinead O'Connor
Sinead fankail
c/o Chrysalis
EMI House
43 Brook Green
London W6 7EF

Optimystic
c/o WEA Records
28 Kensington Church
Street
London W8 4EP

The Orb
c/o Island Records
22 St Peters Square
London W6 9NW

Ozzy Osbourne
c/o Epic Records
10 Great Marlborough
Street
London W1V 2LP

P

Pet Shop Boys
PO Box 102
Stanmore
Middlesex
HA7 2PY

Tom Petty
890 Tennessee Street
San Francisco
California 94107
USA

Pink Floyd
'Brain Damage'
Magazine
c/o Glen Povey
9 Pollard Avenue
Denham
Uxbridge
Middlesex UB9 5JN

Brad Pitt
c/o Triad Artists

10100 Santa Monica
Boulevard
Suite 505
Los Angeles
California 90067
USA

PJ & Duncan
PO Box 122
Ashford
Kent
TW27 9BZ

Prefab Sprout
62 Clayton Street
Newcastle Upon Tyne

Prince
The New Breed
PO Box 858
Old Chelsea Station
New York
NY 10012
USA

Elvis Presley
Official Fan Club
PO Box 4
Leicester
also
Elvis Presley
International Fan Clubs
Elvis Presley
The following branch leaders of the Official Elvis
Presley Fan Club have been elected for the period
ending December 1995. There are branch leaders
in most countries of the United Kingdom and there
is certain to be one in your area. If you've yet to
register with your branch leader send a stamped
addressed envelope to the relevant address and
you will be advised of the club's activities at a local
level.
Avon & Wiltshire
Lyn Vose, 6 Fairway, Melksham, Wilts.
Bedfordshire
Tony Saunders, 168 Gardenia Avenue, Luton, Beds
LU3 2NT.
Berkshire Della Foot, 96 Chiltern Crescent, Earley,
Reading, Berkshire RG6 1AN.

also
PO Box 44
London W1A 4AH

Prodigy
Midi Management
Glen Gyle
205 Vicarage Hill
Benfleet
Essex SS7 1PF

Propaganda
Official Magazine
PO Box 88
Wellingborough
Northants
NN8 1HE
England

Pulp
Pulp People
PO Box 87
Sheffield
S6 2YE

Birmingham Michael Coyle, 15 Handley Grove, Northfield, Birmingham 30.

Borders Margaret Black, 1 Yetholm Mains, Kelso, Rox. TD5 8DB.

Buckinghamshire Vilma Kinney, 11 Plantation Way,Amersham.

Cheshire Val Pettit, 14 Oldfield Road, Wheelock, Sandbach.

Cleveland Stuart Colley, 69 Walter Street, Stockton-on-Tees.

Derbyshire Pauline Torincsi, 3 Crich Place, Hepthorne Lane, Chesterfield, Derbyshire S42 5LY.

Devon M. Wheetman, 37 Ribston Avenue, Hill Barton, Exeter.

Dorset Linda Masters, Burcroft, Nordan Road, Blandford Forum, Dorset DT11 7LT.

Dundee T. B. Lees, The Flounders Inn, 9–11 Erskine Lane, Broughty Ferry, Dundee DD5 1DG.

Edinburgh Kevin D'Arcy, 16 Hawthornbank Place, Edinburgh.

Essex Mike Davis, 15 Dunlin Close, South Woodham Ferrers, Essex.

Wendy Brown, 25 Church Street, Harwich, Essex CO12 3EA.

FifeSean McKenna, c/o Ewan Brande, 17 Keith Drive, Glenrothes, Fife.

Glamorgan (Mid) Chris Hallett, 3 Carswell Place, Gwaun Miskin, Nr. Pontypridd.

Glamorgan (West) Gwyneth Allen, 6 Heol Marien, Chasemont Part Estate, Morriston, Swansea SA6 6 EL.

Glasgow Andy Kane, 6 Dunphail Drive, Brucefield Park Estate, Glasgow G34 0BY.

Gloucester Diane Hill, 3 Lower Quay Street, Gloucester GL1 2JX.

Hampshire Marlene Norris, 32 Ascupart Street, Southampton SO1 1LU.

Hertfordshire Tina Fosdick, 210 Milsmay Road,Martins Wood, Stevenage.

Humberside Mike Hawkings, 18 Euston Close, Bean Street, Anlaby Road, Hull.

Kent David Gabriel, 53 St Patricks Road, Ramsgate, Kent.

Leeds Pat Phillips, 418 Oakwood Lane, Leeds 8.

Leicester Mick Haywood, 40 Hawthorne Street, Leicester LE3 9FQ

Leicestershire (South) Bob Shaw, 12 Orkney Close, Hinckley, Leics LE10 OTA.

London & Home Counties (East) Terry Mailey, 76 Pretoria Road, Leytonstone, London E11.

London & Home Counties (North) Teresa Currie, Uplands, The Warren, Radlett, Herts.

Manchester Dennis Williams, 5 Cambourne Street, Rusholme, Manchester M14 7PH.

Merseyside Maria Davies, 11 Kenilworth Road, Blundellsands, Liverpool.

Norfolk (North) Ellen Knox, Church Bank, Terrington St Clement, Kings Lynn, Norfolk PE34 4NA.

Norfolk (South) Terry Wortley, 3 Colls Road, Norwich NR7 9QZ.

Northern Ireland Michael Mullen, 131 Linn Road, Craigyhill, Larne, Co. Antrim.
David Bill, 44 Ashley Drive, Bangor, Co. Down.

Nottinghamshire David Slack, 59 Wheatgrass Road, Chilwell, Nottingham NH9 4JJ.

Oxfordshire Jenny de Fraine, 49 Marlborough Road, Grandpont, S Oxford OX1 4LW.

Rhondda David Owen, 13 Oakland Terrace, Ferndale, Rhondda, Mid-Glamorgan CF3 4UD.

Shropshire Jan Douglas, 48 Telford Road, Dawley, Telford.

Somerset Paula Fry, 46 Cranhill Road, Street, Somerset BA16 0BZ.

Staffordshire Maureen Handley, 117 Old Fallings Lane, Bushbury Hill, Wolverhampton.

Suffolk Martin Smith,
3 Hervey Street, Ipswich IP4 2ES.

Surrey Clare Jackson,
21 Buxton Lane, Caterham, Surrey.

Sussex Morag Hardinge, 78 Newland Road, Worthing, Sussex BN11 1LB.

Tyne & Wear Leslie Charlton, 6 Croftwell Close, Bleach Green, Blaydon-on-Tyne, Tyne & Wear.
David Trotter, 59 Cambridge Road, New Silksworth, Sunderland, Tyne & Wear SR3 2DQ.

Warwickshire (Mr) Gil Priest,51 Broadway, Cubbington, Leamington Spa West Midlands
Margaret Harris, 38 Highfield Lane, Quinton, Birmingham, Wiltshire
Val Morse, 3 Karslake Close, Eldene, Swindon, Wilts SN3 3SX.

Yorkshire (South) Sonya Bruske, 3 Bramley Grange Way, Bramley, Rotherham S66 0UW.
Dave Zdrenka, 36 Ridgeway Avenue, Dartfield, Nr Barnsley, South Yorks.

European fanclubs

Austria

Elvis Presley Fan Club Österreich, Peter Baumann, Offenes Fach 543, A-1101 Wien.

Belgium Nicole Marechal, Graceland EPFC, 62 Rue Aux Grands Champs,
4950 Beauchamps.
Françoise Geysen, IEPFC, PO Box 266, 1000 Brussels 1.
(Flemish speaking);
International Elvis Presley Fan Club, Hubert Vindevogel, Pijlstraat 15, 2730 Zwinjndrecht.
Denmark
Elvis Presley Fan Club of Denmark,
Kate Jorgensen, Enghave Plads 14, 1640 Kobenhavn V.
Finland
Elvis Presley Fan Club of Finland, Box 21, 03601 Karkkila.
France
Treat Me Nice Elvis Presley Fan Club,
Jean-Marc Gargiulo, 306 Rue de Belleville, 75020 Paris.
West Germany
Elvis Presley Gesellschaft e.V.,Helmut Radermacher, Postfach 1264, D-8430 Neumarkt 1.
Holland Peter Haan, It's Elvis Time, Postbus 27015, 3003 LA Rotterdam.
Always Elvis Fan Club,
Postbus 60, 6990 AB Rheden.

Q

Queen
46 Pembridge Road
London W11 3HN

R

Radiohead
w.a.s.t.e.
PO Box 327
Oxford
OX4 1EY

Rednex
c/o Zomba Records
165–167 High Road
Willesden
London NW10 2SG

Keanu Reeves
c/o Els Boy Ents
7920 Sunset Boulevard
Suite 250
Los Angeles
California 90046
USA

Lionel Ritchie
c/o Tim Simpson
17337 Ventura Blvd
Suite 300
Encino
California 91316
USA

Roaring Boys
2 New Kings Road
Chelsea
London SW6 4NT
England

Robson & Jerome
PO Box 36
Hexham
Northumberland
NE47 9YZ
also
c/o RCA
Bedford House
69–79 Fulham High
Street
London SW6 3JW

Diana Ross
PO Box 69646
Los Angeles
California 90069
USA

Rush
c/o Anthem Records
189 Carlton Street
Toronto
Ontario
MJA2K7
Canada

Cliff Richard Movement
ICRM
PO Box 2BQ
London W1A 2BQ

Cliff Richard Fan Club
Cliff Richard fan clubs affiliated to the ICRM are
independent clubs, but they follow some basic
rules. All clubs distribute 'Dynamite International'
to every member. In addition some clubs have club
bulletins and others a complete club magazine of
their own.
Membership fees are not always the same, as this
depends on what is on offer.
Affiliated clubs don't grant membership to fans not
living in the club's area.
In case you have complaints about your club, or
about 'Dynamite International' first write to your
own club. Only if this doesn't help write to the
ICRM in Amsterdam.

**International Cliff Richard Movement
HQ:**
PO Box 94164
1090 GD Amsterdam
Netherlands
UK information address:
ICRM
PO Box 2BQ
London W1A 2BQ

Cliff Richard Fan Clubs in the UK
Birmingham (also for Staffs): Anthea Jansen, 1
Aldis Road, Walsall,WS2 9AY
Bristol & Somerset: Maureen Neathway, 22 Trent

Close, Yeovil, Somerset, BA21 5XQ

Derbyshire & Notts: Rita Dowding, 173 Pym Street, Nottingham, NG3 2FF

Devon & Cornwall: Sue Collier, 205 Hemerdon, Heights, Chaddlewood, Plymouth, Devon, PL7 3TJ

Dorset: Freda Hector/Maureen Wakefield, 22, Benmoor RoadCreekmoor, Poole, Dorset, BH17 7DS

East Anglia: Sandy McGreish,133 George Lambton Avenue, Newmarket, Suffolk, CB8 0BN

Edinburgh (also for East & North Scotland): Susan Davie, 8 Neidpath Court, Craigievar Wynd, Edinburgh, EH12 8UF

Gloucester & Oxford: William Hooper, 17 Podsmead Road, Tuffley, Gloucester, GL1 5PB

Hampshire: Marion Cunningham, 67 Park Road, Freemantle, Southampton, SO15 3DD

Hereford & Worcester: Nicky Piercey, 12 Monks, Way, Peopleton, Pershore, Worcs, WR10 2EH

Hertfordshire & Bedfordshire: Judy Brewin, No.8, Lloyd Court, 15 The Crescent, Bedford, MK40 2RT

Kent: Helen Jones, 29 Wren Road, Sidcup, Kent, DA14 4LY

Lancashire & Cumbria: Kathleen Fereday, 46 Rydal Road, Lancaster, LA1 3HA

Leicestershire & Northamptonshire: Mrs L. Mowe 148 Roston Drive, Hinckley, Leics, LE10 0XP

Lincolnshire & Humberside: Mrs Julie Leighton, 3 Folkingham Road, Billingborough, Lincs, NG34 0NT

London & Surrey: Janet Manley, 78 Portland Road, Kingston-on-Thames, Surrey, KT1 2SH

Manchester: Sandra J. Hough, 4 Dawlish Avenue, Cheadle Hulme, Stockport, Greater Manchester, SK8 6JF

Merseyside & Cheshire: Wendy Leftwich, Greystones Cottage, 85 Thingwall Road East, Thingwal, Wirral, L61 3UZ

Middlesex & Buckinghamshire: Mrs S.P. Hands, 11 Southview, Downley, High Wycombe, Bucks, HP13 5UL

Northern Ireland: Ann Thompson, 409 Ballysillan, Road, Belfast, BT14 6RE

North East England: Maureen Winn, 29 Rodsley Avenue, Gateshead, Tyne & Wear, NE8 4JY

Strathclyde (also for Dumfries & Galloway): Mrs Evone White, 'Sunnyvista', 2 Beechwood Road, North Carbrain, Cumbernauld, Lanarks, G67 2NW

Sussex: Carole Davies, 18 Westlake Gardens, Worthing, West Sussex, BN13 1LF

Wales: Angela King, 1 Ffordd Penrhwylfa, Prestatyn, Clwyd, LL19 8AD
Warwickshire: Wendy Ashby, 51 Shenstone Avenue, Rugby, CV22 5BL
Isle of Wight: Dawn Nott, 5 Park Road, King's Town Estate, Brading, I.o.W, PO36 OHU
Wiltshire & Berkshire: Sarah & Paul Mullins, St. Teresa's Cottage, Church Street, Tisbury, Salisbury, Wilts
Yorkshire: Jennifer Chatten, 26 Wentworth Drive, Harrogate, Yorks, HG2 7LA

S

Sade
IBC
1–3 Mortimer Records
London W1
also
c/o Epic Records
10 Great Marlborough Street
London W1V 2LP

Mike Scott
Mike Scott Info Society
PO Box 45
Belfast
Northern Ireland
BT7 1WB

Shabba Ranks
c/o Epic Records
10 Great Marlborough Street
London W1V 2LP

Shakespears Sister
c/o London Records
Chancellors House
72 Chancellors Road
Hammersmith
London W6 9SG
England

Shakin' Stevens
158 Camden Road
London NW1 9HJ

Shed Seven
PO Box 777
Coventry
CV7 9BG

Paul Simon
PO Box 32
Kendal
Cumbria
LA9 7NP

Simply Red
1TRB
16 Nurnam Avenue
Sanderstead
Surrey
CR2 0QE

The Simpsons
Fox Broadcasting
PO Box 900
Beverley Hills
California
USA

Sister Sister
39 Chestnut Grove
Kingswood
Clondalkin
Co Dublin
Eire
also
Info Only
PO Box 117
Princeton Junction
New Jersey 08550
USA

Slade
International Fan Club
PO Box 4YD
London W1A 4YD

Snoop Doggy Dogg
c/o East West Records
The Electric Lighting
Station
48 Kensington Court
London W8 5DP

Soldier Soldier
c/o Central TV
Central House
Broad Street
Birmingham
B1 2JP

Jimmy Somerville
c/o London Records
Chancellors House
72 Chancellors Road
Hammersmith
London W6 9SG

Spin Doctors
c/o Epic Records
10 Great Marlborough
Street
London W1V 2LP

Bruce Springsteen
Info Only
PO Box 319
Reading
Berks RG2 8QS
also
c/o Sony-Columbia
10 Great Marlborough
Street
London W1V 2LP

Squeeze
c/o A&M Records
136–144 New Kings
Road
London SW6 4LZ

Star Trek
Official Fan Club
PO Box 111000
Autora
Colorado 89942
USA

Lisa Stansfield
c/o Arista Records
423 New Kings Road
London SW6 4RN

Rod Stewart
PO Box 4000
Los Angeles
California 90046
USA

Barbra Streisand
Barbra Streisand
Association
17 Adrian Place
Peterlee
County Durham
SR8 5SR

Sting
94 Kensington Park
Road
London W11

Suede
PO Box 23384
London W11

T

Take Note
PO Box 169
Camberley
Surrey
GU15 2GS

Tank Girl
PO Box 435
London SE1 4SP

Tears for Fears
c/o Epic Records
10 Great Marlborough
Street
London W1V 2LP

Terrovision
Total Vegas
PO Box 516
Bradford
BD12 0YY

Tip Top Club
PO Box 2095
London W1A 1LN

TLC
2625 Piedmont Road
Suite 56-161
Atlanta
Georgia 30324
USA

**International Tina
Turner Fanclub & Info
Center**
Elle Denneman,
President
Postbox 41
1720 AA Broek op
Langedijk
The Netherlands

Top of the Pops
Ticket Unit
BBC TV Centre
Wood Lane
London W12 7SB
England

**Toad the West
Sprocket**
c/o Sony-Columbia
10 Great Marlborough
Street
London W1V 2LP

Trevor and Simon
c/o Children's BBC

BBC TV Centre
London W12 7RJ

U

U2
Info Only
PO Box 48
London N6 5RU

UB40
Info Service
PO Box 117
Birmingham
B5 5RD

2 Unlimited
c/o CBA Artists
PO Box 1495
1200BI
Hilversum
Netherlands

Ugly Kid joe
PO Box 6061-204
Sheremanoaks
California 91423
USA

Ultimate Kaos
The Kaos Club
PO Box 276
London E2 7BW

Utah Saints
c/o London Records
Chancellors House
72 Chancellors Road
Hammersmith
London W6 9SG

V

**Jean-Claude van
Damme**
c/o ICM
8899 Beverly Boulevard

Los Angeles
California 90048
USA

Tim Vincent
PO Box 1249
Wrexham
Clwyd
LL13 0ZD
Wales

Vic and Bob
Vic Reeves Big Night
Out
Official Fan Club
PO Box 297
London SE7 7LU

Warren G
c/o Keesaa Harris
Ral Violator Records
160 Var Cick Street
New York
NY 10013
USA

Paul Weller
c/o Go! Discs
72 Blacklion Lane
London W6 9BE

Wet Wet Wet
Splash
14-16 Spierswharf
Port Dundas
Glasgow
G4 9TB
Scotland

Whigfield
PO Box 276
London E2 7BW
also
c/o London Records
Chancellors House
72 Chancellors Road
Hammersmith
London W6 9SG

Kim Wilde
PO Box 202
Welwyn Garden City
Herts
AL6 0LT

Bruce Willis
c/o Triad Artists
10100 Santa Monica
Blvd
Los Angeles
California 90068
USA

Stevie Wonder
4616 Magnolia Blvd
Burbank
California 91505
USA

World Party
World Party Fanmail
Chrysalis Records
EMI House
43 Brook Green
London W6 7EF

X

The X Files
PO Box 3138
Nashua
New Hampshire
03061-3138
USA

Y

Neil Young
Appreciation Society
2A Llynfi Street
Bridgend
Mid Glamorgan
Wales

Paul Young
PO Box 4UB
London W1A 4UB

Z

ZZ Top
PO Box 19744
Dept TN
Houston
Texas 77224
USA

Zig & Zag
c/o The Big Breakfast
2 Lock Keepers
Cottages
Old Ford Lock
London E3 2NN
England

Fan Club Focus
(King Of Clubs)

Elvis Presley is still very much alive! That is the clear message I got when I spoke to Todd Slaughter, Secretary of The Official Elvis Presley Fan Club.

'We have in excess of 20,000 active members with clubs established in every country of the world, including China, The Soviet Union and even one on the Falkland Islands,' stated Todd proudly.

Quite clearly Elvis Presley is still, almost 20 years after his death, big business. Still King of the Charts, having had a new hit in the charts every year since 1956 – that's a total of 40 consecutive years of hit singles!

So how long could the club justify its existence from the material available?

'Firstly, Elvis is not a finite product. He is dead, he is not going into the recording studio, they are not making films about him any more, but they are making videos. There are 26 Elvis Presley videos available at present which is more than any other artist. Also RCA have a lot of unreleased material which on their present frequency of releases will see me out.'

Todd's affinity with Elvis goes back over 30 years when upon leaving school he worked with an Elvis Presley nutcase. He soon joined the club. Telstar had just been launched and Elvis's manager, Colonel Parker, insisted that due to Elvis's fear of flying this was the only way for him to reach a worldwide audience. Todd promptly collected a quarter of a million signatures to encourage a satellite appearance and Jimmy Saville took the petition to America.

All seemed set, only for the Colonel at the last minute to announce 'If the signals go to the moon, I haven't got an agent there and the little green men will be watching for nothing and that's not what I want.'

Todd then started to write for 'Elvis Monthly', which is now in its 36th year, and on the 16th August 1967 he was asked if he would like to run Elvis's fan club.

'So I did. There were no members at all when I took it over. If you read 'Elvis Monthly' and sent a s.a.e. you simply got a membership card!'

'Elvis Monthly' proved the perfect vehicle for Todd to launch and establish this most respected of fan clubs. Through Todd's devotion and tireless enthusiasm the Club now boasts some 50 branches nationally. Each year the Club organises an annual charity convention, a sponsored weekly members' holiday and, of course, the annual August pilgrimage to Memphis.

If the loyalty of Elvis Presley fans is renowned, then the activities of this club are legendary. Truly and fittingly this is . . . a King of Clubs.

* U.K. membership costs £7.50 annual subscription plus £1.50 p&p. Each member receives in addition to a membership card a bimonthly full colour magazine and various other benefits, plus an extensive social entertainment programme through the Club's Travel Service, including a week long 'Elvis Holiday Festival' in one of the highly acclaimed Pontin's Holiday Villages – plus access to what must be unquestionably the largest array of memorabilia of any artist in the world.

Send an s.a.e. for further details to:-
The Official Elvis Presley Fan Club
PO Box 4
Leicester LE3 5HY

Did You Know . . . ?
Long and Short of Rock

Here is the long and short of the rock world. Diminutive Prince is a full 13 inches shorter than Simon Le Bon, whilst Jason Orange and Howard Donald dwarf Jimmy Somerville by nearly a foot! Quite clearly talent isn't measured in inches.

5'1"	**Prince, Jimmy Somerville**
5'3"	**Cindy Lauper**
5'4"	**Madonna**
5'5"	**Kim Wilde**
5'6"	**Andy Taylor, Tina Turner**
5'7"	**Mark Owen**
5'8"	**David Bowie, Annie Lennox**
5'9"	**Michael Jackson**
5'10"	**Bruce Springsteen, Paul McCartney, Gary Barlow**
5'11"	**George Michael**
6'0"	**Jason Orange, Howard Donald**
6'1"	**Boy George**
6'2"	**Simon Le Bon**

Rockin' Record

Rory Blackwell, former Beach Boys drummer and one-time member of Lord Rockinghams XI, who had a No. 1 hit with 'Hoots Man', played his way to a world record when he hammered out 'When The Saints Go Marching In' using a staggering 314 different instruments in just 84 seconds! The instruments ranged from a tiny harmonica to an 11-foot alpine horn. The veteran rocker hit the final note by driving head first through a drum!

Rory said, 'It was great fun.'

Did You Know . . .?

Now Here's Some . . .

Earth-shattering news

Super group U2 really sent the shock waves rippling out at a concert in Brussels, Belgium, when they drew such a thunderous reception from their fans that it was actually picked up on the local seismograph, establishing them as the first group ever to register an earthquake on the Richter Scale!

Did You Know . . .?

Shortest Titles

The shortest title ever is 'U', recorded by American Loni Clark, which reached No. 28 in the 1994 UK charts.

The shortest title for a No. 1 hit was 'If' by David Gates for Telly 'Kojak' Savalas and a lesser hit for comedy due Yin and Yan.

Janet Jackson made No. 14 in 1993 with the same title.

Records, Records, Records!!!!

Singles – Most No.1 Hits

17 – Beatles (including one with Billy Preston)
17 – Elvis Presley
13 – Cliff Richard
9 – ABBA
8 – Rolling Stones
7 – Madonna

Most Top Ten Hits

63 – Cliff Richard (including one with Sarah
      Brightman, Phil Everly and The Young Ones)
55 – Elvis Presley
33 – Madonna
29 – Michael Jackson (including two with Paul

McCartney and 11 with The Jacksons)
25 – Beatles

Most Consecutive Top Ten Hits
32 – Madonna
26 – Cliff Richard
24 – Beatles (their first 24 releases)
23 – Elvis Presley (his first 23 RCA releases)

Albums
Most No. 1 Albums
12 – Beatles
9 – Rolling Stones
8 – ABBA. Queen. Led Zeppelin
7 – David Bowie. Paul McCartney/Wings.
     Rod Stewart
6 – Elton John. Cliff Richard. Elvis Presley.
     Bob Dylan

Most No. 1 Albums
in a Calendar Year
Only two acts have achieved the feat of getting three
albums to No. 1 in one year.
1965 – Beatles (*Beatles For Sale*; *Help*; *Rubber Soul*)
1972 – T.Rex (*Electric Warrior*; *Prophets Seers/My
     People Were Fair*; *Bolan Boggle*)

Most Consecutive
No. 1 Hit Albums
11 – Beatles
8 – ABBA. Led Zeppelin
6 – Rod Stewart

Only three acts have
knocked themselves off
the top of the charts.

1963 – Beatles	*With The Beatles* replaced *Please Please Me*.
1964 – Beatles	*Beatles For Sale* replaced *A Hard Day's Night*.
1965 – Bob Dylan	*Bringing It All Back Home* replaced *The Freewheelin' Bob Dylan*.
1974 – Mike Oldfield	*Tubular Bells* replaced *Hergest Ridge*.

Singles
Most Weeks in the Charts
1145 – Elvis Presley
1100 – Cliff Richard
508 – Elton John

Others of Interest
437 – Rod Stewart
434 – Beatles
397 – Paul McCartney/Wings
357 – Queen
269 – Prince
188 – Pet Shop Boys
139 – Simply Red. George Michael
131 – A-HA
116 – INXS
101 – Guns 'N' Roses

Hot Tips for the Fame Game

Rock's highway is paved with gold – or so they say. But getting your hands on all that lovely loot can be a very frustrating business for the aspiring pop star. If you manage to clamber aboard the musical roller-coaster, the rewards are beyond the dreams of avarice. Estates in Epsom, penthouses in Paris, mixing with millionaires in Monte Carlo – a jet-set life of never-ending parties or seclusion and senility. The choice is yours. Make it to the top of the pop pile and there will be no need to cry 'open sesame'; the door will be forever open to a lifestyle once only afforded to the likes of kings and queens.

But before you rush off to find that 'golden key', convinced you have both the talent and shrewdness to survive in the jungle of pop, beware the sharks that idle in the tempting Caribbean blue sea . . . dolphins, as Paul King will tell you, are a very rare species in these waters!

The Wham! story is a perfect example of the piracy that so often occurs on the high seas of the pop waves. After George Michael and Andrew Ridgeley had had several smash hit singles and an equally successful album, selling millions of records in the process, they were still having to survive on £40 a week!

The most vulnerable moment in the life of anything is at the beginning as the predators lie in wait for the naïve and ambitious struggling to secure a foothold on the ladder to fame.

Managerless, hungry for success, many grab at the first opportunity to bridge the great divide between the backwaters packed with small fry, furious to get noticed, hopeful to be extracted from the swim and given the diploma of approval, and that all-important first recording contract.

The inadequacy of Wham's! first contract with Innervision left them practically penniless, unable to afford the luxury of a taxi home after a prestigious *Top of the Pops* performance.

What a performance, what a game – play your cards right, throw the correct dice and you climb the ladder past the door of the dreaded A & R office into a land where all your whims and desires are catered for, everything is possible. But make one false throw, one mistake in this fickle tinsel world, and you slither down the snake in this board game that promised the winner a crock of gold.

Those who remain on board can, at their leisure, reflect on some of the prizes picked up by other winners.

Paul McCartney, who has written or co-written more million-selling records than anyone else, puts in excess of £25 million a year into his piggy bank. This is the equivalent of almost half a million pounds a week or £75,000 a day!

David Bowie can pick up a cool £1 million for just one concert.

Whilst these are extremes, even with a modicum of success the pickings are rich indeed. The dole one day, the Dorchester the next. Remembering that success is no respecter of talent, what price will our 'Hot Tips' have to pay for a share in all this perpetual wealth?

A total commitment of nothing less than 101 per cent, a continual intense single-mindedness which is all-consuming, obliviousness to all except the one objective, one goal – to get to the top and stay there. To live the life of royalty in a goldfish bowl world starved of privacy!

These are the qualities and sacrifices needed to win the . . . Fame Game.

PRO

TILES

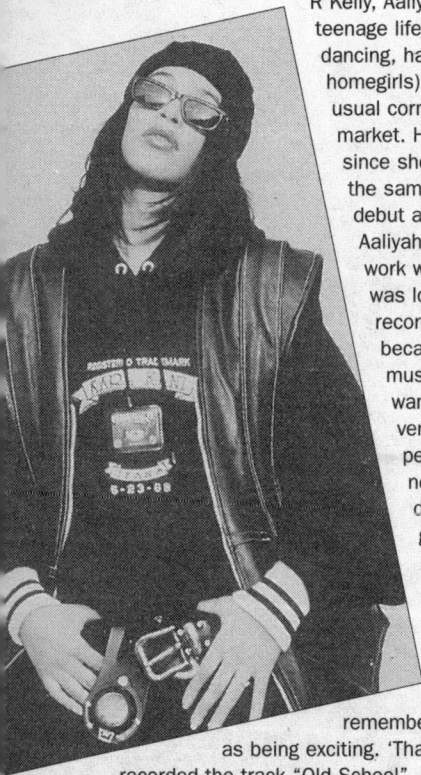

Aaliyah

In this age of designer soul, numerous plastic-voiced divas have been created in the studio. Although their shimmy is booming, these youthful singers often lack the one element that transforms a whisper to a soulful cry: passion. On her debut disc, *Age Ain't Nothing But A Number*, Aaliyah (ah-lee-yah) proved that the ner jill swing movement can move beyond freeze-dried vocals and boring grooves.

Produced and written by the multi-platinum balladeer R Kelly, Aaliyah's songs of teenage life (falling in love, dancing, hanging with da homegirls) transcends the usual corniness of youth market. Having known R Kelly since she was 12 years old – the same year his own debut album dropped – Aaliyah was very excited to work with the balladeer. 'I was looking forward to recording with R Kelly because he makes the music that kids my age want to hear. He's a very spontaneous person meaning you never know what direction his music is going to take you.'

Age Ain't Nothing But A Number was recorded in R Kelly's hometown of Chicago and Aaliyah remembers the first session as being exciting. 'That first night we recorded the track "Old School". Outside it was cold and snowing, but inside the studio was hot!' R Kelly and Aaliyah's combination of old school and new led to a remake of an Isley Brothers song that Aaliyah feels is one of the best on the album. The remake of their classic pillow talk ballad 'At your Best (You Are Love)' is the perfect homage to the old school. The soundscape that R Kelly has created for this track recalls Stevie Wonder's production for Minnie Ripperton or Phil Spector's wall of sound. The album's first single, 'Back and Forth', which upon release charged up the pop and R&B charts, is a head-boppin', hip-swaying celebration of boogie nights in Aaliyah's hometown of Detroit. 'When I'm not recording or practising, I love to go to parties or out dancing with my friends,' she explains. With a booming bass that has been constructed with jeep sound systems in mind, 'Back and Forth' will have the residents of Motown dancing in the streets once again.

The title track is yet another song of passion that revealed a musical side of Aaliyah that she hasn't experienced personally. 'Romance is not something I've had a lot of experience with, but it's a subject I've thought about. On that song I want to explore what life would be like for a younger girl to be in love with someone older. In my mind I see her talking to her friends, who say, "Girl, don't you know age ain't nothin." And then they would all laugh.' In keeping with the album title, the teenager demurely refuses to tell her age. 'I don't want people to start trippin' on how old I am. I just want them to enjoy the music.'

A student at the newly built Detroit High School for the performing art, Aaliyah is the first professional to emerge from its doors. 'I've sang in many talent shows, performed at weddings, I've even sang Gladys Knight. This is something I've wanted to do since I was a small child.' Her determination towards her recording career doesn't stop her from excelling in school and she manages to maintain straight As, despite her busy schedule.

Although her next album is merely a concept in her mind, Aaliyah says, 'Maybe next time I'll do a little writing and/or producing. Who knows, I might even try doing some rapping.' She laughs, noting Naughty By Nature, 2Pac and Wu-Tang Clan as her favourite rappers.

Aaliyah's *Age Ain't Nothing But A Number* proves just that. Her incredible vocals and youthful street appeal combine to create an album that both propels R&B music forward and harks back to the old school sound at her roots.

Welcome to the next level of soul.

Ace Of Base

It was like a fairy tale. An unknown quartet from the Swedish city of Gothenburg by the name of Ace Of Base completed a number of rough mixes for an album, and offered them to everybody – but no record company wanted them. Now, where have I heard that before? Finally, a label was found and the rest is history.

The album *Happy Nation* sold some 19 million copies worldwide! It is by far the most successful debut of all

times, and Ace Of Base is the only Scandinavian band to reach the No. 1 position in both the American singles and LP charts. Prior to steamrolling the United States, Ace Of Base had already waged a phenomenal campaign, conquering Europe with the crisp cheerfulness of singles such as 'All That She Wants' (a huge No. 1 hit in Britain and across the world), 'Happy Nation' and 'The Sign'.

That first album was two years ago. And as is well known, miracles are always a one-time affair. But that is not the case with Ace Of Base, as they proved with their follow-up album, 'The Bridge' (Nov. 1995). The harmonies make their way even more directly into the listener's ear, the sound is comprised of even more layers. Only one thing is noticeable: a trace of melancholic longing pervades the album – giving it the necessary gravity and depth.

'It could be,' admits Jonas Berggren, one half of the male half of the group and the brother of the singers

Jenny and Malin, 'that the underlying mood on *The Bridge* is more measured, and perhaps more solemn than on our debut album. You can't sell 19 million albums without that fact having an influence on the rest of your life. Clearly, a lot has happened during the two years. Things we didn't even dare dream of in the past. Suddenly you're in the public spotlight. That's a completely new experience, and it has naturally influenced the songs on the new album.

'But I would not call it a melancholy or a resigned album. I think it's more that our songs have matured, just like we have. In our eyes, *The Bridge* is an adult album. Perhaps the ballads do sound more wistful than on *Happy Nation*, but then again the few up-tempo numbers turned out even faster than on our debut album. I think that's a fair compensation.'

The four did not feel under any sort of pressure while recording the new album. 'I think we handled it properly,' explains Jonas. 'We took a long break before getting down to recording *The Bridge*. You need the time to digest all that happened in the last exciting year before your head is clear for a new project. That's why it took almost two years to complete the album. We wanted to approach the new CD relaxed and free of any pressures.'

However, their phenomenal and surprising success did have its effect on the four, even if they did always present themselves with effervescence and a disarming friendliness to media representatives and the public. 'Now I understand young bands that become superstars overnight and then flip out,' Ulf reveals. 'Some nights I was pretty close to becoming paranoid, because I felt as if I was being constantly observed by a camera. Your whole life suddenly becomes transparent. But we solved the inner conflict by coming closer to each other as a band.

'Ace Of Base no longer consists of three siblings and a friend, but now comprises a strong family of four. Of course, success also has its good side: we hung out at a lot of interesting parties, we met a lot of our childhood idols, and lead exciting, fulfilling lives. At the same time, we have never forgotten where we came from and who we are. I think that Ace Of Base is a good example of how four people can be successful without flipping out. Instead, we look at the future optimistically and hope to be able to make a few more records that we are proud of.'

It's an ace game, set and match.

Bryan Adams

| Date of Birth: | | **11.5.59** |
| Star Sign: | | **Scorpio** |

Best Record Positions:

1985	'Run To You'	No. 11	12 weeks
1991	'Everything I Do (I Do For You)'	No. 1	24 weeks
1992	'Thought I'd Died And Gone To Heaven'	No. 8	7 weeks
1993	'Please Forgive Me'	No. 2	16 weeks
1994	'All For Love'	No. 2	13 weeks

Baby–D

When BABY D shot to No. 1 in the national charts
with their classic dance anthem, you knew this was
not a sudden success story. The band had already
entered the U.K. dance chart at No. 1 a full two years
before topping the national charts. They had been
constantly playing live since they formed in 1990,
when they performed their set live – real instruments,
BABY D's stunning vocals, and innovative street
dancers, unlike many 'PA' dance bands who mime
their way through a few songs. Needless to say their
hard work paid off, resulting in a fiercely loyal fan
base across the country.

The writer/producer Dice, although an integral part of

BABY D, wasn't with the band on their summer live dates but was soon back at the near-legendary Production House (where BABY D make their hits) concentrating on making more hits. Old friend and Production House ally Claudio Galdez took his place on keyboards, windsynth, and on stage.

The new line-up gigged in April when fans caught them at Sound City supporting The Prodigy and The Chemical Brothers. July through August saw BABY D embark on a nationwide tour.

Their single '(Everybody's Got To Learn Sometime) I Need Your Loving' is an old song (well, about 12 years old) originally performed by The Korgis. Most of the song is unrecognisable, except perhaps for the unmistakable chorus!

Released May 1995, the single was produced and mixed by Nino with vocals produced by Dice. Other mixes will be The Masters of House mix and a Neil McLelland (co-producer of The Prodigy) mix, whilst there is a separate 'No Sell Out' jungle mix 12#ai by Ray Keith through the Production House, coupled with a D-SP mix.

BABY D – you can be my fantasy!

Backstreet Boys

Backstreet Boys are the new teen sensation sweeping America. Originating from Kentucky and Florida, the boys – Kevin, Brian, A.J., Howie and Nick – have been working hard on the road for the past 18 months and recording their debut album. Kevin (22) and Brian (20) are cousins both born in Lexington where they spent most of their teens singing in church choirs and clubs and venues in the area. During family visits they harmonised classic doowop and contemporary hits, their biggest influences being Boyz II Men and Jodeci.

A.J. (17), Howie (21) and Nick (15) were all born in Orlando and met up at auditions for musical theatre, television and films. All three had solid credentials as solo performers. It was at these auditions that the boys began singing a cappella to pass time.

It was Kevin who brought the band together. He decided to leave Kentucky, to go to Orlando (where he got a job in Disney World) and devoted his time to becoming a professional singer-songwriter. It was there that he heard of 'these guys' who spent their time harmonising at auditions. He arranged a meeting and they all got on so well they decided to team up. Kevin called the cousins back home in Kentucky and he immediately joined Kevin and the rest of the boys to create Backstreet Boys.

Signed to Jive in early 1994 the boys went into the studio, with producers Vit Rein and Tim Allen, recording their debut album that included their hit single 'We Got It Going On'.

These Backstreet Boys could well be to the fore for years.

The Beatles

Date of Birth:

Paul McCartney	18.6.42
Ringo Starr	7.7.40
John Lennon	9.10.40
George Harrison	25.2.43

Star Sign:

Paul	Gemini
Ringo	Cancer
John	Libra
George	Pisces

Best Record Positions

1963	'From Me To You'	No. 1	21 weeks
1963	'She Loves You'	No. 1	31 weeks
1963	'I Want To Hold Your Hand'	No. 1	21 weeks
1964	'Can't Buy Me Love'	No. 1	14 week
1964	'A Hard Day's Night'	No. 1	13 weeks
1964	'I Feel Fine'	No. 1	13 weeks
1965	'Ticket To Ride'	No. 1	12 weeks
1965	'Help'	No. 1	14 weeks
1965	'Day Tripper/We Can Work It Out'	No. 1	12 weeks
1966	'Paperback Writer'	No. 1	11 weeks
1966	'Yellow Submarine/ Eleanor Rigby'	No. 1	13 weeks
1967	'All You Need Is Love'	No. 1	13 weeks
1967	'Hello Goodbye'	No. 1	12 weeks
1968	'Lady Madonna'	No. 1	8 weeks
1968	'Hey Jude'	No. 1	16 weeks
1969	'Get Back'	No. 1	17 weeks
1969	'Ballad of John and Yoko'	No. 1	14 weeks

John Lennon:

1980	'(Just Like) Starting Over'	No. 1	15 weeks
1980	'Imagine'	No. 1	13 weeks
1981	'Woman'	No. 1	11 weeks

Paul McCartney:

1977	'Mull of Kintyre/ Girls School'	No. 1	17 weeks
1982	'Ebony and Ivory'	No. 1	10 weeks
1983	'Pipes of Peace'	No. 1	12 weeks
1989	'Ferry 'Cross The Mersey'	No. 1	7 weeks

George Harrison:

| 1971 | 'My Sweet Lord' | No. 1 | 17 weeks |

Ringo Starr:

1971	'It Don't Come Easy'	No. 4	11 weeks
1972	'Back Off Boogaloo'	No. 2	10 weeks
1973	'Phoo Grapa'	No. 8	13 weeks
1974	'You're Sixteen'	No. 4	10 weeks
1992	'Weight Of The World'	No. 74	1 week!

Mary J. Blige

Call her the 'Queen of Hip-Hop Soul'. Call her a New Jack diva. Call her the New Chaka, the New Aretha. Call Ms. Blige what you wish. But ask Mary what she calls herself and she'll probably say 'a homegirl who wants to sing'. *My Life*, her long-awaited follow-up to the 1991 double platinum debut *What's the 411* – which earned her household name status in the hip-hop nation as well as world tours and non-stop airplay – is a testimony to that simple wish.

Whereas *411* was all about jeep-beats and in the pocket vocals, the autobiographical *My Life* finds the beloved alto belting and crooning over a sandscape of freeflowing jazz chords, middle-Eastern background harmonies and atmospheric funk grooves and sounding more polished and confident vocally than ever. Executive-produced by Sean 'Puffy' Combs and Andre Harrell, *My Life* takes you back to classic 70s R & B, when Quiet Storms were born, when real instruments provided the funk and when Mary J. Blige began discovering that life was a song worth singing. It was an era when, as Mary simply says, everybody sounded good'.

'This album has more of an old feeling,' she explains. 'It feels like the music I grew up on – Stevie Wonder, Aretha Franklin, Chaka Khan, Gladys Knight, Mavis Staples. I haven't lost the street vibe, but it was time for me to do this. It's more emotional to me.'

The emotion comes on strong, no doubt due to the fact that Blige makes her debut as a lyricist. The album documents the life and mood swings of a homegirl looking for love, searching for her inner peace and singing for her salvation. The first two lines of the bridge of her funky-yet-philosophical first single 'Be Happy' sum it up best: 'I just wanna be so happy/But the answer lies in me?'

'In that song, I'm singing that for everybody. A lot of people aren't happy and that's all they want. People will cramp your style because they're too afraid to do what they want to do. But it's up to you to do what you have to do to be happy.'

If some of the tracks on *My Life* sound familiar, you're not imagining things: they are. 'Be Happy' is based on vamp (replayed live) from 1983; 'Mary Jane' borrows its brass line from the Mary Jane Girls' 1983 hit 'All Night Long'; and the title track is anchored by the chord progression of Roy Ayers' Quiet Storm classic 'Sunshine'. It was Mary's decision to anchor her signature stylings and spiritually tinged lyrics with some of the grooves she grew up with.

'When I was on tour with Jodeci in London I played 'Sunshine' everyday,' she remembers. 'It reminds me of my Daddy. But I think that people want to hear real music nowadays. They want to hear the feeling you get when the harps come in Curtis Mayfield's 'Gimme Your Love' [which is re-invented lyrically as 'I'm The Only Woman']. It's like being in water . . . you can actually see blue.'

Blur

The history of BLUR can be dated as far back as 1980, when Damon Albarn and Graham Coxon met as schoolboys in the city of Colchester. Damon, a Londoner by birth, was raised by liberal, artistic parents (his father had been connected to the psychedelic rock bank Soft Machine in the late 1960's). Both Damon and Graham showed considerable musical talent as teenagers, with Damon winning a 'Young Composer' competition and Graham playing saxophone in local bands.

In 1988, Graham, by now a student at Goldsmiths' College in London, introduced Damon to Alex James, a friend of Graham's at Goldsmiths'. They formed a band called Seymour – with Damon on vocals (and occasional keyboards), Graham on guitar, Alex on bass and an old friend from Colchester, Dave

Rowntree, on drums. After playing a dozen or so shows in and around London, they re-named the band Blur in 1989. The personnel has not changed since, or ever looked likely to.

After signing to Food Records in February 1990, the first release from Blur was the single 'She's So High' that October, a melodic and wistful song very typical of early Blur: languid-sounding, with yearning harmonies and strange, goofy bass-playing.

The story really began to gather speed with the next single, 'There's No Other Way', a big hit in Britain in the spring of 1991. This song saw BLUR working for the first time with legendary producer Stephen Street (The Smiths, Morrissey, The Cranberries). Stephen has produced the bulk of Blur's music ever since, including 'The Great Escape'. Blur's debut album 'Leisure' released in August 1991, was an enjoyable – if not especially cataclysmic – collection of songs with an intriguing triad of musical influences: Syd Barrett's early Pink Floyd, the explosive guitars of My Bloody Valentine and vocal harmonies reminiscent of 'Revolver'– era Beatles. A number 7 hit in Britain, 'Leisure' is nevertheless not very typical of Blur's music nowadays, A complete change of attack was announced by the single 'Popscene' in March 1992: furiously-paced, acerbic, with blaring horns over punky guitars. Songwriter Damon Albarn had undergone a key transformation, from reticent by-stander to biting social commentator, and BLUR greedily stockpiled the songs that would make up their sophomore album, the critical break-through 'Modern Life Is Rubbish'. Names from a piece of graffiti scrawled on a wall near London's Marble Arch, 'Modern Life is rubbish', May 1993, represented an absolute sea-change. Flying in the face of all the music being created by their peers, it thumbed a pop encyclopedia of England (Julian Cope, XTC, Madness) in an effort to combat the then-uniformly grunge dynamic of contemporary rock. It was alternately seen as a brave and foolhardy move. However, the album's witty and proudly parochial songs (variously bolstered by use of string sections, brass sections and cor anglais) aimed for – and achieved – a quintessential English sound not heard since the 60's heyday of The Kinks. The songs' subject matter was just as English, yet it was far from nostalgic or wistful. Modern Life, as seen by Albarn, was a barren land walled in by advertising hoardings, with almost nowhere to hide from mental pollution.

These were ideas developed on the third BLUR album, 'Parklife', April 1994, which took a slow, analytical stroll through England and filmed the country's people on an unintrusive Camcorder. There they were: eating pizza, dreaming of Disneyworld, off to Greece on holidays, watching pornography. Some of them were deluded. Some were time-honoured "cheats", in the tradition of Keith Talent, the anti-hero of Martin Amis' apocalyptic novel London Fields. Some were zombies (the glue-sniffing star of 'Jubilee') Many more were simply having fun while it lasted.

Influences (Kinks, Bowie, Smiths, Magazine) to create a palette that was inspirationally fresh and unashamedly colloquial in an age of garbled mutterings. If you played the album right through, it was like turning the dial of a radio: from disco to glam, to punk to queasy listening.

'Parklife' entered the British album charts at Number 1, and BLUR have been the cheery potentates of their homeland's pop scene ever since. Recently — pleasingly Ray Davies of The Kinks has voiced his enthusiasm for their work. He and Damon sang 'Waterloo Sunset' together on the British TV show, The White Room.

Some months in the making 'The Great Escape' is Blur's worldwide coming of age. Its musical range outstrips traditional pop. banjo, Mellotron, curdled waltzes and zonked-out keyboards all take a bow in the band's ingenious arrangements. It will sound novel in whichever country it is heard. And the album's topics, too, reach far beyond England, perhaps because that small country can no longer hold the band's increasingly restless attention, or perhaps because the 'Great escape', with all its ominous interpretations, is not feasibly something that will take place on land... but in space, in international dreamtime, on water...

Boyzone

It all began in November 1993. Three hundred young men gathered in Dublin to audition for a place in the line-up of Ireland's first teen sensation. Shane, Mikey, Keith, Ronan and Stephen were the lucky five to be selected, and Boyzone were formed.

Since then things have just got better and better for the boys, two of whom were car mechanics before being chosen for the band. It wasn't long before Polygram signed them up and the hunt for a debut single was on. 'Working My Way Back To You' (the classic Detroit Spinners track) became the obvious choice. Within weeks of release it had reached No. 3 in Ireland. Suddenly Boyzone was a household name, and the band were no longer able to walk in their home town without being chased by their frenzied fans.

For the follow-up, their manager Louis Walsh flew the band to London to record with Take That writer Ray Hedges. The best track to come from that session was 'Love Me For A Reason' by the Osmonds. On its first week of release in Ireland, the song entered the charts at No. 3. Within two weeks it had given the boys their first No. 1.

By this time, Polydor UK could no longer ignore the signs of Boyzone mania and snapped them up immediately. It didn't take long for the hysteria to catch on in the UK. The band's first performances in the UK were on the Smash Hits Roadshows and by the end of the tour their popularity was so immense Boyzone were voted Best Band On The Road by their new fans. This accolade catapulted them on to the Smash Hits Pollwinners' Party and an audience of over 11 million. That night 'Love Me For A Reason' entered the charts at No. 11.

To follow were a series of TV appearances, magazine front covers and extensive airplay, establishing Boyzone as the hottest tip for 1995. 'Love Me For A Reason' climbed to No. 2 in the charts. When Boyzone were first put together, band member Keith Duffy quipped, 'When we get to do *Top of the Pops* and we're on the front cover of *Smash Hits*, that's when we know we've arrived.'

Following their sell-out UK tour and debut No. 1 album Boyzone are, as I write, releasing their fourth single, 'Father and Son'. Written by Cat Stevens, this is a beautiful rendition of the song which went down so well with their fans on tour. It is also a very special record for the group as it was sung by Ronan at his first audition for Boyzone!

Boyzone are currently on a sell-out promotion tour of Europe and the Far East.

Boyzone are:
Ronan Keating.

Ronan is the youngest member of Boyzone, born 03.03.77. Ronan left school to join the band, despite his mother's initial apprehension. 'She was worried about drugs and all the late nights.' Despite this, the other band members think Ronan is the most mature in the band and he often makes all the decisions.

Stephen Gately.

Stephen was born 17.03.76. 'I'm a typical Piscean, sensitive and shy.' Stephen admits that his first ambition was to become an actor but couldn't turn down the chance to be in Boyzone. He has an obsession with Smarties and Jelly Tots and thinks Kylie Minogue is just 'gorgeous'.

Shane Lynch.

Shane's a Cancerian and was born 03.07.76. 'I used to be a mechanic and sing all the time in the garage. The other guys said I was really good and talked me into auditioning for Boyzone.' Shane reluctantly admits to having a pet snake which he feeds live goldfish to.

Michael Graham.

Mikey is the oldest member of Boyzone and the most serious. He was born 15.08.72. Most of the writing is done by Mikey and his favourite singers are Sting and Eric Clapton. 'I like restoring old cars. I used to do kickboxing but I gave that the chop – ha, ha!'

Keith Duffy.

Keith was born 01.10.74. Keith left college, where he was studying architecture, in order to join Boyzone. He is described by the rest of the band as 'someone who puts up this hard guy image, but underneath it all he's really soft and sweet.' He used to be into Gothic music and wear long black hair.

Discography
Singles

28.11.94	'Love Me For A Reason'	No. 2
17.04.95	'Key To My Life'	No. 3
31.07.95	'So Good'	No. 3

Albums

| 21.08.95 | *Said And Done* | No. 1 |

The Brotherhood

No doubt one of The Brotherhood's biggest assets is their longevity – rather than being an overnight creation, the group have a hefty ten-year history to draw on. The current three-piece, original founding member Shylock, fellow rapper Spyce and DJ Dexter, is only the latest line-up in a long stream of changes that have happened to The Brotherhood since originally forming as a teenage collective of rappers, break dancers and graffiti artists in 1985. Although the current line-up is only three years old, the group members share a common history dating back to the mid-80s breakdancing scene in London's Covent Garden. 'We're just a posse of boys from the same era who've now gelled for the 90s,' says Spyce. 'We're like brethren, it's not like we just met yesterday. That's made the whole work vibe easy; there's no ego, we build tunes like brethren.' The Brotherhood also reflect the multi-racial nature of British rap with the song 'One 3', the flip side of the double A-sided debut single for Virgin which explains the group's racial make-up and their attitude towards it. 'That track is about the nature of The Brotherhood but it could be about anybody. Things like that make no difference to us, so why should they make any difference to anyone else. If things can be done together in music, why can't they be done together everywhere else?' says Shylock.

Musically, a key influence on The Brotherhood set-up has been their producer, The Underdog. Best known as a remixer for the likes of Massive Attack, U2, House of Pain, The Gravediggaz, it was he who released The Brotherhood's initial records in the early 90s on his Independent Bite It label. Generally regarded as one of the UK's best and most innovative hip-hop producers, The Underdog has provided the group with a cutting-edge musical backdrop for their raps whilst also managing to keep in step with The Brotherhood's pro-British attitude. Wherever possible, The Underdog has taken his samples from old British records, ingeniously creating modern hip-hop from sounds taken from the unlikely source of late 60s progressive rock groups such as Soft Machine and King Crimson.

The Brotherhood are ready to get out and support their music in the live arena. Live performance has always been the Achilles' heel of British rap groups in the past, but the group are confident about performing. 'The burden will fall upon my shoulders to pull it all together,' says The Brotherhood's DJ Dexter, 'but we're definitely going to come live off the decks rather than tape. I don't want to be the dumb DJ pushing the DAT machine.' In the live arena, the group are refreshingly lacking in hang-ups about their music crossing over to non-rap audiences. As Dexter puts it, 'We've got the potential to rock the college crowd and the indie crowd. I'm not prejudiced – I'll talk to anyone.'

Dina Carroll

If the musical year of 1993 was notable for one fact above all others, it wasn't the breakthrough of Eurodance music, nor the revival of the 7inch single or even the ever-increasing volatility of the UK charts: the one abiding statistic that stands head and shoulders above all these was that a young singer/songwriter by the name of Dina Carroll released her first album *So Close* in January and 12 months later that same record had become the biggest-selling UK debut of 1993.

These two facts only tell a small part of this phenomenal story. The album yielded six huge hits – 'Ain't No Man', 'Special Kind of Love', 'This Time', 'So Close', 'Express' and 'Don't Be A Stranger' – and these in turn were crowned at Christmas by Dina's glorious rendition of the Andrew Lloyd-Webber song 'Perfect Year'. Echoing the sentiments of the song itself, Dina thus capped the year with two concurrent Top 10 UK hits, a million-plus selling album and a triumphant UK tour already under her belt.

In retrospect, there were (and Dina is the first to admit this) no obvious early signs of impending greatness: the daughter of an American father and British mother, now famously born in the back of a taxi cab, Dina described herself in a recent interview as 'an introverted child, horribly lacking in confidence'. However, her impromptu vocal recitals at family get-togethers gradually convinced both Dina and those around her that a career in music offered better possibilities than her childhood ambitions of becoming a ballerina or gymnast.

This process of confidence-building bore its first real fruit in 1990 when Dina was asked to contribute a lead vocal to Quartz's cover of the Carole King classic 'It's Too Late'. A Top 10 hit, the record gave Dina both the experience and exposure needed to contemplate a solo career. More importantly, it brought her voice to the attention of millions, and soon after the break-up of Quartz, Dina signed a solo deal with A&M Records. If ambition enters the equation it does so here, with Dina at last bringing to bear those musical influences that had filled her early years, namely The Temptations, Isley Brothers, and Aretha Franklin. Her goal was to produce and deliver a timeless soul/dance record that would, while reflecting current dance strains, have more spiritual kinship with these vocal icons from her past.

Co-writing with producer Nigel Lowis, the result was a brilliant hybrid of urban dance and classic soul. The songs themselves were utterly timeless, the imprint of CJ Mackintosh on the dance mixes completely true to their time. These two factors combined to propel Dina's debut single 'Ain't No Man' into the UK charts and Dina's voice into the hearts of thousands.

The story thereafter is now well documented; suffice

to say that the true significance of Dina's success has since been borne out by a host of major accolades, not least a Brits Award in February for 'Best Female Artist', but also with three awards at the International Dance Awards, a Variety Club Award for 'Best Performing Artist' and a nomination for the increasingly prestigious Mercury Music Prize Album Of The Year. The dramatic success of her first UK tour – described variously as 'a triumph' (*The Guardian*) and 'a delight' (*The Times*) – will undoubtedly be regularly repeated.

On a personal note, I still clearly recall taking this shy Cambridge girl (and her mother) with the sultry looks, an engaging line in self-deprecation and a voice that puts her supposed American peers to shame, to her first record company audition at Red Bus. With no musical backing she just opened her mouth and sang! Verdict – 'Great voice but not commercial enough'.

Fortunately, this is a case where success was a respecter of talent. I for one am delighted she hung on in there and will undoubtedly reap her due commercial award.

Phil Collins

| Date of Birth: | 31.1.51 |
| Star Sign: | Aquarius |

Best Record Positions:

1982	'You Can't Hurry Love'	No. 1	16 weeks
1984	'Against All Odds'	No. 2	14 weeks
1985	'Easy Lover'	No. 1	12 weeks
1988	'A Groovy Kind Of Love'	No. 1	13 weeks
1989	'Another Day In Paradise'	No. 2	11 weeks
1993	'Both Sides of The Story'	No. 7	5 weeks

Phil has had 183 weeks in the charts with Genesis

Culture Beat

Culture Beat – Jay Supreme and Tania Evans – won the 1993 ECHO award for most successful band abroad. Their single 'Serenity' sold 4.5 million worldwide; the album sold 1.4 million. Amazingly the songs from that album were featured on a staggering 20 million compilations worldwide.

The single 'Mr Vein' reached No. 1 in seven countries, including the UK, and was a Top 10 smash hit all over the world. It was also the first single to go to No. 1 in the UK, selling over one million copies, without a 7#ai format. Definitely a culture that can't be beaten.

De'lacy

De'lacy vocalist Raine La Sitter is a New Jersey Performing Arts School graduate with a degree in English, and a registered nurse! In fact, all members come from professional backgrounds – De'lacy Davis and Gary Griffin were both police officers whilst Glen Branch was a telecommunications technician.

Somewhere there is a formula for chart success, as promised by their autumn 1995 release 'Hideaway', a solid classic song with great backing and of course Raine's incredible vocal delivery.

There's no hiding the potential of De'lacy, they could prove simply unstoppable.

Del Amitri

It could be argued that Del Amitri's huge and enduring appeal, both in Europe and in America, rests on truly classic virtues – timeless pop songs, written, recorded and performed with such attention to detail they should come ready-wrapped. Yet to those who've watched the band's inexorable rise from mid-80s jangling guitar hopefuls to fully-fledged worldwide chart regulars, there's considerably more to this Glaswegian four-piece than meets both the eye and ear.

Even when the brilliant *Waking Hours* emerged in 1989, with its echoes of vintage rock bands like The Faces and Neil Young, Del Amitri's lyrical perspective was always decidedly homegrown. Bittersweet love songs ("Kiss This Thing Goodbye"), tales of suburban torpor ('Nothing Ever Happens') and urban stagnation ('Move Away Jimmy Blue') gave voice to a malaise endemic in late 80s Thatcherite Britain. 'Making the grimly grey seem toe-tapping bright' was how one writer viewed it, arguably the best encapsulation of Del Amitri's appeal.

The 1992 follow-up *Change Everything* continued to make the grey seem bright, the downbeat seem positively full of possibilities. The lead-off single 'Always the Last To Know' brought the band chart success throughout Europe, and songs like the plaintive 'Be My Downfall' and the ironic 'Just Like A Man' confirmed Justin Currie's status as a world-player par excellence.

Then came *Twisted*. Some time in the making but worth every second of the wait, it added a discernible new dimension to Del Amitri.

Marcella Detroit

As a singer and songwriter, Marcella Detroit has been exploring characters for almost as long as she can remember. She has taken the stage with legends, provided words and music for some of the most respected performers of her generation, and been at the heart of one of the most imaginative and theatrical pop success stories of recent years – Shakespears Sister. Now comes her most challenging and rewarding role to date, and in it she plays . . . herself.

'It's a little confusing and frightening at first, but ultimately the most liberating thing I've ever done,' she says of the writing and recording of a much-anticipated solo album, currently in the final stages of production at London's Olympic Studios. 'Over the years I've written with or for so many other people, always focusing on what they wanted. Now, suddenly, it's "OK Marcy, who are you and what do you want to say? What are the things that are important to you?" And the great thing is how easy and natural it's all been, now that I'm finally concentrating on me.'

It all began with 15-year-old Marcy Levy's involvement

in bands on the club scene in her native Detroit – the city is so central to her musical evolution that she took on its name for professional use. Two years later, having left school, she moved to Tulsa, Oklahoma. There she became part of a loose collective of writers and musicians that included bassist Carl Radle, a former member of Delaney and Bonnie Bramlett's backing band who was hired by Eric Clapton to play on the album *461 Ocean Boulevard*. Through Radle, Marcy herself was then conscripted as a backing singer on the resultant world tour.

After five years based in the city, she moved on to Los Angeles, where she focused on writing songs both for herself and other artists, and began a lengthy period of acting tuition and performance. 'Initially I got into that because I felt so exposed on stage,' she explains. 'I was very withdrawn, and felt I needed to do something to free myself of the fear I had when performing. And I ended up loving it – it was like therapy. I learned so much about myself, as well as about acting. It helped me to grow up a lot, which in turn was good for my singing and my writing.'

Throughout the well-documented career that has followed, Marcy can justly claim to have helped expand the territory open to women artists through her category-defying sound and arresting, theatrically-inspired performances. And this interdependence between music and acting remains central to her new work: 'I think of Marcella Detroit as a character with different facets who's integrated into me,' she says. 'Hence all the songs are very personal, and based on real rather than fictitious experiences. I put my emotions directly into the lyrics, making them an extension of me. The personality explored within them is my own.'

Celine Dion

There's no shortage of hyperbole when describing the meteoric rise of Celine Dion. Barely four years ago she was a virtual unknown outside her native province of Quebec. Today she is an international superstar with her first two English-language albums selling millions throughout the world.

In Canada alone, Celine has sold over seven million

albums in both French and English, with her debut English-language album, *Unison*, yielding four Top 10 singles and over 400,000 sales and capturing for her the Juno Awards for Female Vocalist of the Year. There followed a tribute album to Quebec songwriter Luc Plamondon called *Dion Chante Plamondon* which went double platinum overnight, enjoyed considerable sales in English Canada and went gold in France. Celine's international breakthrough came with the soundtrack to the animated Disney hit movie *Beauty and the Beast*. The song went to No. 1 in the U.S., Top 10 in the U.K. and garnered an Academy Award for Best Song. *Beauty and the Beast* formed the cornerstone for Celine's second English-language album called, simply, *Celine Dion*. That album produced five hit singles including 'Love Can Move Mountains', 'Water From The Moon', 'If You Asked Me To', 'Did You Give Enough Love' and 'Beauty And The Beast', which also earned Celine a Grammy Award. In Canada the album went six times platinum, in the U.S. platinum, and in Australia gold.

The woman who was once Quebec's best-kept secret has now appeared on the Academy Awards, twice at the Grammys, twice at the American Music Awards and countless times on the *Tonight Show*. Last year she hosted the Juno Awards and won for the third consecutive year Female Vocalist of the Year.

The Colour Of My Love, her third English-language record, built on the success of the soundtrack to the hit film *Sleepless in Seattle*, for which Celine sang the theme song 'When I Fall In Love'. That album went double platinum in the U.S., platinum in Canada and triple platinum in the UK!

Think Twice sold more records in the UK in 1994 than any other artist or group. She is the only female artist ever to stay at the top of the single and album charts for five weeks in a row, so joining a hall of fame shared only with the Beatles, Cliff Richard and Elvis Presley. Celine also joins Whitney Houston, Whigfield and Jennifer Rush as one of only four women to sell more than one million copies of a single. The record also won the award for Best Song Musically and Lyrically at the 1995 Novelles Awards. Celine Dion is an exceptional singer who sings exceptionally well and no one has to think twice about that!

Dodgy

Dodgy are not unfamiliar with the mood swings and fickleness of the British music press, where bands are lauded to the hilt one moment, discarded contemptuously the next. Despite this, critical acclaim greeted both Dodgy's debut album in '93 and last winter's *Homegrown* opus. It was only hit singles that were absent. How different the scene is now: four consecutive hit singles, sell-out tours, and praise from almost all sides have confirmed Dodgy as a real success story. The star turn at Blur's Mile End Show, the highlight of Glastonbury, the all-smiling TOTP's performers – things could hardly be looking better. *The Dodgy Album*, produced by Ian Broudie, offered ample evidence of a band following a grand tradition of melody/guitar-led home-grown pop. Songs like 'Water Under The Bridge' and 'Lovebirds', bearing hooks as big as houses, are pop classics in any era and gave the band widespread radio play and an ever-increasing band of followers. But there was more: to some it rested with the still-flourishing, multi-flavoured monthly chaos that was the Dodgy Club. To others it was the band's phenomenal, loose-limbed (but never baggy) ability to conjure up groove-led anthems like 'Summer Fayre', 'Easy Way' or even 'Worth The Blood'.

With a live show that veered from the truly inspirational to occasional moments of wilful recklessness, Dodgy are a musical enigma. Neither ephemeral press darlings nor workmanlike jobsworths, they continue to work their musical furrow, all the time picking up new converts. Whether the current vogue for all things English in pop music is another case of media manipulation or a genuine grass-roots 'happening', it will make little or no difference to Dodgy's place in the scheme of things. Like the proverbial square peg in the round hole, Dodgy's future success will ultimately rest with those who can still recognise great pop records without being constrained by the tyranny of current opinion. That, in short, is what makes Dodgy so special: hip they may not be, classic they most definitely are.

Jason Donovan

Date of Birth: 1.6.68
Star Sign: Gemini

Best Record Positions:

1989	'Too Many Broken Hearts'	No. 1	13weeks
1989	'Sealed With A Kiss	No. 1	10 weeks
1989	'When You Come Back To Me	No. 2	11 weeks
1989	'Every Day (I Love You More)'	No. 2	9 weeks
1990	'Rhythm Of The Rain'	No. 9	6 weeks
1991	'Any Dream Will Do'	No. 1	12 weeks

Dreadzone

Greg and Leo were the drum and bass backbone of 80s cultural collision Big Audio Dynamite before going on to form Screaming Target with Don Letts, and it was during the making of their critically acclaimed album that they met up with Tim Bran, who had been making his name as a producer and remixer. This strengthened the creative nucleus resulting in a totally individual sound that was immediately snapped up by Creation in 1993.

Dreadzone orbit the world of music, scanning the positive elements to feedback into a unique sound that reflects cultural diversity in the UK. Their much-feted debut recording *360 Degrees* was a dub-charged satellite. *The Times* described it as hitting 'a spot only occupied previously by The Orb'. It included the singles 'The Warning' and the Morricone-inspired 'The Good The Bad And The Dread'. They also contributed the single 'Fight The Power' (a *Melody Maker* single of the week) to *Taking Liberties*, the album released in support of the anti-Criminal Justice Bill movement.

Dreadzone

The years of (BAD) experience at the cutting edge of live technology launched Dreadzone into a live field of their own. Real drums and bass in harmony with machines underpin a sound of clash on stage, with dub mixing and trance 'making a sound that is both emotionally and physically breathtaking' (*Melody Maker* '94). This energy was captured on a limited edition album *Performance* released at the end of 1994 after a year of extensive touring. Now with the recent addition of Chris Bran supplying a live mix of visual cut-ups, camera work and image fragmentation, Dreadzone consolidate their reputation as one of the most uplifting *live* experiences of the mid-90s. Dreadzone are in a position to challenge the accepted profile of dance and related groups with a forthcoming album that defies category and live presence that thrives on rock and roll energy.

East 17

East 17 formed a few years ago in Walthamstow when Anthony Mortimer, inspired by a heady brew of soul, R&B and Prince-style pop, gathered together a selection of mates from school and his streetwise gang and went home studio barmy. Having convinced ex-Pet Shop Boys/Bros supremo Tom Watkins that he knew what he was rapping about, Anthony managed to land his band a deal with London Records in March 1992. East 17's debut single was 'House Of Love' (August '92). A swaggering slice of primetime dance-angled pop,it was the first (potentially) across-the-board single since EMF's 'Unbelievable'. East 17 didn't land themselves a support slot on a University tour and face being bottled off by 'indie' bigots. Instead they went on a tour of the nation's schools and managed to become embroiled in a media-invented teenybop rivalry with Take That!
'House Of Love' hit the UK Top 10. Proving that a bit of cockernee action never hurt foreign climes, it also went to No. 1 in Israel, Sweden and Finland and invaded the charts of Germany, Austria, Denmark and Australia. Better still, when the floor-pumping turntable-gliding follow-up 'Gold' (Nov '92) infiltrated the Swedish chart at No. 3, 'House Of Love' was still No. 1.
Vox called it Lad Pop. Quite right too, but no amount of dismissive critical shoulder-shrugging can disguise

the fact that East 17 are trying to say something. 'Gold' is a philosophical overview of what is really important in life; 'I Disagree' details a list of injustices as long as a rubber arm. It's a hard life and Anthony Mortimer is well aware of its inherent firmness. 'The rest of the world is probably laughing at us, but I'll argue until the day we die that we are singing about something serious,' says the singer. 'If we encourage this generation of kids to chill out then maybe we're leading the way, in a few years time the world will be a better place to live in. We hope.'

After a change of pace with the slinky, bedsheet-staining 'Deep' (January '93) which dived into the UK charts peaking at No. 5, it is hardly surprising that *Walthamstow*, the album, thoroughly confused the media masses. *Select* noted the 'horribly infectious choruses', whilst *Smash Hits* came to the glad but inevitable conclusion that 'It's hard for any pop fan to dislike East 17.' And of course they're right.

When East 17 launched *Walthamstow* (February '93) it went straight into the UK album charts at No. 1. Alongside the Mayoress of Waltham Forest in Walthamstow High Street, over 3,000 schoolgirls clambered over the fruit 'n' veg stalls to grab a piece of the action.

'Slow It Down' was East 17's next release (March '93), which followed nicely in the footsteps of their previous singles by brightening up the UK charts. Then came a cover of the Pet Shop Boys classic 'West End Girls' in East End style (June 93) – another UK hit peaking at No. 11

With the release of 'It's Alright' (November '93) as their Xmas single, East 17 stepped up a gear. Not only was this their biggest single so far, but it's chart life seemed never-ending, spending over 3 months in the UK Top 40 after its release, with seven of those weeks in the Top 10 peaking at No. 3. Meanwhile *Walthamstow* went platinum in the UK, selling over 300,000 copies.

'Around The World' (May '94) was the first single to be taken from East 17's second albums witnessed the beginning of a maturer, wiser, more soulful yet still enthusiastic, East 17. 'Around The World' the single was accompanied by a month full of live sell-out tour dates (their first) in the UK. '*Around The World*' burst straight into the charts and spent a throbbing three weeks at No. 3. This was followed by a writing and recording period for their second album and another new single peaking at No. 7 entitled 'Steam' (which was remixed for the B-side by Carter

USM, long-time fans of East 17).

Next came the release of their second album, also entitled *Steam* (October '94) which revealed a maturer East 17 (but still with that Walthamstow edge). It went double platinum in the UK alone by the beginning of 1995 and in only five months almost matched the 1.8 million worldwide sales of *Walthamstow*.

The album was followed with another single release, 'Stay Another Day', (which Tony wrote for his brother). 'Stay Another Day' became East 17's first British No. 1 single and stayed at the top of the UK charts for five weeks notching up the Christmas 1994 No. 1 slot and selling over a million singles in the UK alone by January 1995.

East 17 followed this up with another single in March 1995 entitled 'Let It Rain' (another Top 10 hit!). Then came another live European tour through summer 1995 and another hit single coinciding with the tour – 'Hold My Body Tight' peaked at No. 12 in the UK charts in June. The tour was a huge success which included two sell-out dates at London's Wembley Arena.

The lads returned to the studio to write album No. 3. All concerned were so pleased with the material that the single 'Thunder' was quickly put into place for release in October, with the album *Up All Night* released in November 1995.

Discography:
UK Singles:

'House Of Love'	Aug. '92	No. 10
'Gold'	Nov. '92	No. 28
'Deep'	Jan. '93	No. 5
'Slow It Down'	Mar. '93	No. 13
'West End Girls'	June '93	No. 11
'It's Alright'	Nov. '93	No. 3
'Around The World'	May '94	No. 3
'Steam'	Nov. '94	No. 7
'Stay Another Day'	Nov. '94	No. 1
'Let It Rain'	Mar. '95	No. 10
'Hold My Body Tight'	May '95	No. 12

East 17? They came, they phoooaaarghed, they conquered.

Erasure

Date of Birth:
Vince Clarke   **3.7.61**
Star Sign: **Cancer**

Best Record Positions:

1986	'Sometimes'	No. 2	17 weeks
1988	'Crackers International'	No. 2	13 weeks
1990	'Blue Savannah'	No. 3	10 weeks
1991	'Chorus'	No. 3	9 weeks
1991	'Love To Have You'	No. 4	9 weeks
1992	'Abba Esque'	No. 1	12 weeks
1994	'Always'	No. 4	9 weeks
1994	'Run To The Sun'	No. 6	5 weeks

Eternal

It is sometimes hard to pinpoint the exact moment of a coming of age. But for Britain's No. 1 girl group, Eternal, the realisation that things had moved on came on the day they recorded the track 'Power Of A Woman', which was to be the first single from their new album of the same name. 'Of all the songs we heard and all the songs we co-wrote it was the most powerful both lyrically and musically,' says Kelle Bryan. 'The title just stood out and we thought "That's what we are about", the power of a woman is a strength, an inner quality that we all have. It's something that we've discovered more so in ourselves over the past two years.'

In 1993 Eternal were a new South London quartet wondering what it would be like to join their heroes and heroines such as Stevie Wonder, Michael Jackson, Sound of Blackness and Aretha in the Hall of Fame. They didn't have to wait long. When their debut single 'Stay' shot straight into the national charts at No. 4 not only did they convince thousands of pop fans, but also captured the new spirit of British urban soul and gave the homegrown dance scene the vocal power and visual personality it craved. However, the four girl members of the group were no overnight sensation; sisters Easther and Vernie Bennett were finely honed vocal talents from a church background and Kelle Bryan and Louise Nurding had perfected their performing talents at Italia Conti stage school. When they signed to Oliver Smallman and Denis Ingoldsby's First Avenue Records the ground was laid for a first-class R&B act. Their debut album, *Always & Forever*, attracted U.S.A. producers like Bebe Winans and Scott Cutler as well as the U.K.'s Steve Jervier and Nigel Lowis. There was no way anyone was going to face these veterans of Whitney Houston and Al Green through the studio glass unless they knew exactly what they were doing! The results from the album are now the stuff of legend. SIX Top 15 hit singles, SIX No. 1 dance hits, FOUR Brits nominations, a Silver Clef award, an American chart success, a sell-out tour of Europe with Take That, a gold record in Japan and fantastic success in places as far away as south-east Asia. *Always & Forever* has now sold nearly two million copies worldwide!

Faith No More

1982

Bordin (born 27.11.62 in San Francisco), Buttum (born 1.7.63 in Los Angeles) and Gould (born 23.4.63 in Los Angeles) form Faith No More.

1983

Chuck Mosely joins as vocalist.

1984

Jim Martin (born 21.7.61 in Oakland, CA) joins as guitarist.
Faith No More sign to Mordam Records, a San Francisco independent label run by Ruth Schwarz.

1985

Release first album *We Care A Lot*.

1986

The band sign with Slash Records, a Los Angeles-based independent label. Anna Stadtman is the A&R person responsible for making the deal. This deal later develops into a split between Slash and Reprise

Records, an arm of the Warner (U.S.) company. In the U.K., London Records, from the PolyGram group, sign the band.

1987
April: The album *Introduce Yourself* is released.

1988
Feb: Faith No More play in the U.K. for the first time.

May: A second U.K. tour sees Chuck Mosely's final shows with the band. He is dismissed. A 'critics choice' in the U.K., the band cannot break the U.S.

Dec: The single 'We Care A Lot' charts in the U.K. at No. 53.

1989
Jan: Mike Patton (born 21.1.68 in Eureka, CA) joins as new singer.

June: 'The Real Thing' is released.

Sept: Start a five-week West Coast U.S.A. tour with Metallica.

Oct: Another U.K. headline tour.

Nov: European headline tour.

1990
Jan: Tour the U.S. with Voi-Vod and Soundgarden. 'EPIC' charts in the U.K. at No. 37, the band do another U.K. tour.

Feb: The Grammy nomination for Best Heavy Metal/Hard Rock performance. They don't win.

April: Another U.K. tour sees the single 'From Out Of Nowhere' reach No. 23 in the U.K. charts.

July: 'The Real Thing' goes U.S. gold (500,000).

August: Release a concert video, 'You Fat Bastards – Faith No More Live At The Brixton Academy, London'. Headline the Reading Festival in England and tour Australia.

Oct: The 'EPIC' single hits the U.S. top 10 (No. 5) and the U.K. Top 30 (No. 25) after being reissued. 'The Real Thing' is U.S. platinum (1,000,000 sales) reaching the No. 11 spot. It moves to double platinum in 1991.

1991
Feb: U.K. released live album *Live At Brixton* reaches No. 20 in the U.K. album charts.

March: Win five Bammie (Bay Area Music Awards) awards.

1992
June: Release *Angel Dust* LP, immediately go on tour with Guns 'N' Roses in Europe.
July: Single 'Midlife Crisis' reaches the U.K. top 30 (No. 18).
Nov: *Angel Dust* reaches U.S. gold (500,000 sales).
Dec: Tour the U.K./Europe with L7.

1993
Jan: Tour of U.S. with Babes in Toyland and Kyuss.
Feb: The band's cover of The Commodores' single 'Easy' reaches No. 3 in the U.K.
July: After another successful European tour, the band headlines 50,000 capacity Phoenix Festival in the U.K.

1994
Jan: After a month of wrangling, Jim Martin is fired.
Aug: After months of searching for a guitarist, Trey Spruance joins. He is Patton's bandmate in their other project Mr Bungle.
Sept: Andy Wallace is confirmed as the producer of FNM's forthcoming album, marking the first time an album has been done without Matt Wallace at the helm.
Sept/Oct/Nov:
  The band commence with, and complete, the recording and mixing of *King For A Day . . . Fool For A Lifetime*. It is recorded in Woodstock, NY at Bearsville Studios and mixed in Manhattan.
Dec: New guitarist Spruance decides that touring for long periods of time would be too much for him. The band replaces him with Dean Menta, who did the entire *Angel Dust* tour as a keyboard tech.

1995
Feb: 'Digging The Grave' is released as the first single from the new album on the 27th.
Mar: On the 13th, *King For A Day . . . Fool For A Lifetime* is released worldwide.

Faith No More are nobody's fool.

Fine Young Cannibals

One Monday morning in 1985, it seemed that half of Britain was talking about an unknown three-piece combo who had appeared on *The Tube* pop show the previous Friday night – all over England, people wanted to know who had written this great tune, and who the singer was with the soulful voice and striking appearance.

A few weeks later, 'Johnny Come Home' by The Fine Young Cannibals was in the higher reaches of the chart – a truly remarkable debut.

It all started when ex-Beat members Andy Cox and David Steele were looking for 'A Voice'. In a search which took them halfway across the world and back, they finally found what they were looking for in the shape of Roland Gift, singing with a soul/R & B band in Finsbury Park!

The band were only into their sixth month when they appeared on *The Tube* – a TV debut which resulted in excited A & R men banging on their doors, wielding promises of 'name-your-price' advances, just begging the threesome to sign on the dotted line. They eventually signed to the fledgling London label.

'Johnny Come Home' was followed by another single, 'Blue', and a debut LP, simply titled *Fine Young Cannibals*, in December 1985. The New Year came, and FYC released a cover of the Elvis classic 'Suspicious Minds', giving the song an entirely new treatment, and giving the band their first hit stateside. A U.S. tour followed in the latter part of 1986 and it was here that they met up with Barry

Levinson, the director responsible for the classic cult movie *Diner*.

Levinson asked FYC to write the score and four songs for his new film *Tin Men*, starring Danny De Vito and Richard Dreyfuss. So when the tour ended they flew to Los Angeles to score the movie. It opened in the summer of 1987 and featured a cameo performance by the band, appearing as a 60s soul group playing in a bar.

When they returned to the U.K., Fine Young Cannibals recorded 'Ever Fallen In Love' at the request of Jonathan Demme for his movie *Something Wild*. It was released in March 1987 and went on to be another Top 10 smash.

Though he had only been seen on screen for a few minutes, such was the impact of Roland's celluloid debut in *Tin Men* that he was offered a large variety of acting roles. Nothing interested him until he was approached to appear in a film being made by the team responsible for *My Beautiful Laundrette* - director Stephen Frears and writer Hanif Kureishi, who had seen him on *Top of the Pops*. FYC had no more commitments until work was due to begin on the second LP, so Roland was able to accept the offer. *Sammy and Rosie Get Laid* opened worldwide in autumn 1987.

But when the second album was finally released in February 1989 – nearly three years after their debut album –and it shot to No. 1 in the national charts. Entitled *The Raw and The Cooked*, the album proved to be an eclectic combination of dance tracks and soul ballads that surprised and delighted the most discerning and sometimes cynical audience.

A second single from the album, 'Good Thing', was released in April and also reached the Top 10 (No. 7). *The Raw and The Cooked* album has remained in the U.K. charts since February 1989.

The band completed a sell-out tour of the U.S.A. in late '89 where they were feted by the likes of Madonna and Michael Jackson in the rock world, and Jack Nicholson and Warren Beatty from the 'aristocracy' of the film business.

Returning from the States in late October, FYC performed a short stint of British shows culminating in three sell-out dates at Brixton's Academy! At the same time London Records released the haunting ballad 'I'm Not The Man I Used To Be' and in December released 'The Raw and The Cooked' video compilation: five classic tracks including '2 Men, a Drum Machine and a Trumpet'.

January 1990 saw the boys being nominated for awards at home and in the U.S.A. where they have been nominated for Grammys for Best Single ('She Drives Me Crazy'), Best Performance By A Group, and Best Album. In the U.K. the BPI have nominated FYC in three categories: Best Band, Best Male Vocalist and Best Album.

A stack of nominations and 4 million albums later and you ask 'has it gone to their collective heads?' No way. Roland spent Christmas and the New Year in New Zealand (where he bought some land) and returned to rehearse his part as Romeo in Shakespeare's *Romeo and Juliet*. It's not the Hollywood film nor a low budget British picture but a stage performance with the small but beautiful – and highly regarded – Hull Truck Company!

Andy and Dave have also been busy with Price Paul (of De La Soul) re-mixing a 'club' version of the track 'I'm Not Satisfied' – plus writing and producing a track for Monie Love.

So a year of achievements for the band; but not really a gamble that suddenly paid off. When asked why it took so long to make the album David explained, 'We could have written an album in a few months just to satisfy either the record company or the public, but if you want to satisfy yourself and produce something worthwhile . . . then it takes a little longer.'

Welcome home!

Michelle Gayle

Born in north London (she's NOT an Eastender by birth) in a house that forever echoed to the mellow sounds of her parents' soul collection – and with countless weekends of reggae that filled her grandmother's house – Gayle's musical roots run deep. Gladys Knight, The Ohio Players, and Al Green colliding with Bob Marley, Dennis Brown and Sugar Minot – the aroma of Jamaican spices from Scandals Cafe – the London rain – the long summers filled with street-dub – the Harlesden traffic jams and the mix of cultures was breeding a wider outlook on life for this twenty-something street-diva.

Yet, raised on rap, this buffalo girl spent days 'just killing time with a mat and beatbox'. She laughs. 'General Levy lived across the road and round the corner we've got MC Juice, and mom used to work over at Omar's Indie label. People like MC Mell'O and Monie [Love] they were my home-boys and girls!' She beams proudly. 'Man, I grew up with all that!' Nucleus, Mtume, Plant Rock, The Treacherous Three, Public Enemy at the Electric Ballroom, Camden; Gayle's diet of hip-mix and hip-hop and street soul are as natural a blend as the music she made with her first real group, Romor Phus. It was rough and ready, but always a necessary sideline to the daytime pressure of acting and singing that her stage school imposed.

Five years on and the Gayle-force is gathering. Spotted by the label behind S.W.V., Omar and Jade, Gayle delivered an unstoppable groove set in the form of her gold album Michelle Gayle which was released in October 1994. Hip-Hop soul? Street New jill swing? Call it what you will. This excellent debut album featured a plethora of outstanding songs including her first single 'Looking Up', a record which came with a credibility tag others lacked, storming into the national charts during the summer of 1993 peaking at No. 11.

For the recording of the second single, 'Sweetness', Michelle took a plane to Los Angeles to meet its songwriter Narada Michael Walden (Whitney Houston, Aretha Franklin fame). The result is a chocolate-coated musical treat which reached the dizzy heights of the No. 4 position in September 1994 and sold over 300,000 copies. The third single, 'I'll Find You', was an exquisite ballad climbing to Top 20 status. The fourth single, entitled 'Freedom' reached No. 16 in May 1995, establishing Michelle as one of the U.K.'s most successful soul divas. The inspired fifth single, 'Happy Just To Be With You', arguably her best to date, reached No. 11 in September 1995. With everyone from Narada Michael Walden to David James to Steve Jervier and Simon Climie in on the secret, Michelle has proved that she's not just another puppet on a very short string, writing and co-writing over 40 per cent of the album. 'I like to talk about things that really matter. Sure, love is something that we all experience, but the album is about real life, y'know, real people.'

Gun

When Gun emerged in the summer of 1989 with their highly acclaimed album debut *Taking On The World*, they were rightly judged as one of the finest bands to emerge from Scotland in the past 20 years. Top 40 singles like 'Better Days', 'Money' and 'Inside Out' confirmed their arrival and an incendiary live show enhanced their reputation across Europe. Indeed, the Gun sound began to hit the mark in some unlikely quarters – in 1990 Gun were invited by fellow Glaswegians Simple Minds to perform in front of 72,000 fans at Wembley Stadium, and as if this wasn't enough later that year Gun were also chosen (at Mick and Keith's specific request and from over 70 bands) to open for the Rolling Stones on their Urban Jungle world tour.

Gun followed this up with the hard-hitting *Gallus* album in 1992, its title a Glaswegian term loosely meaning 'dead cool'. The album saw the band broaching new musical territory. Its no-frills approach had them charting once more with blistering, guitar-driven rock songs like 'Steal Your Fire', 'Welcome To The Real World' and 'Higher Ground'.

And now, after some time out and a streamlining of personnel, Gun are back. To shape a collection of songs into the form of an album, then stamp it with an assured title like *Swagger*, takes more than just bravado or confidence. But it's aptly named, because Gun have produced their most focused and cohesive work to date.

Gun play it loud, but never sacrificing melody for volume. The fiery rock song 'Don't Say It's Over' with its anthemic chorus is a memorable example.

Elsewhere, the hard-assed, grunge rap of 'Something Worthwhile', punching its way off the turntable with the ferocity of a prizefighter, will be the envy of every street-smart homeboy in the U.S.A. Wait till they hear it's rapped by a Scots-Italian, Dante Gizzi!

Yet Gun also have a softer side, best displayed on the flawless rock ballad 'The Only One', which might well be the best song Neil Young never wrote. Rock is dominated by songs about unsuccessful relationships, but from its wailing harmonica to Rankin's tortured vocals, 'The Only One' proves that songs about love-gone-bad always have the real emotional edge.

Swagger had a brash edge backed up by songs of quality and integrity which perfectly sum up the Gun ethic. The title itself comes from a lyric: 'cool kinda swagger/and lips like Jagger'. It sounds just right.

Guns 'N' Roses

Date of Birth

Axl Rose	6.2.62
Slash	23.7.65
Rose McKaggan	5.2.64

Star Sign:

Axl	Aquarius
Slash	Cancer
Rose	Aquarius

Best Record Positions:

1989	'Paradise City'	No. 6	9 weeks
1989	'Sweet Child'	No. 6	9 weeks
1989	'Patience'	No. 10	7 weeks
1991	'You Could Be Mine'	No. 3	10 weeks
1992	'November Rain'	No. 4	5 weeks
1992	'Knockin On Heaven's Door'	No. 2	9 weeks
1993	'Ain't It Fun'	No. 9	3 weeks
1994	'Since I don't Have You'	No. 10	6 weeks

Haddaway

Haddaway's initial success in Britain came in March 1993 when 'What Is Love?' reached No. 2 in the charts. Simultaneously it reached No. 2 in Germany, No. 9 in America and No. 1 just about everywhere else on the globe!! Since then, Haddaway has gone from strength to strength. The follow-up singles to 'What Is Love?' had equal success: 'Life' reached No. 6, and 'I Miss You', a gentle but electrifying ballad, No. 9. The final release from his debut LP *Haddaway – The Album* was 'Rock My Heart', which also reached the No. 9 spot. The album went gold in the U.K., selling in excess of a quarter of a million copies.

The Europop genre has not been noted for producing artists with staying power, yet Haddaway's career has already lasted three healthy years due mainly to his rich mix of superb dance tunes and sophisticated ballads and a vocal and musical dexterity not often seen. His music is characterised by warmth, strength and fun.

It is hardly surprising that Haddaway achieves such a global feel in his songs. Born in Tobago he moved to Washington DC at the age of nine. He grew up to the sounds of Louis Armstrong which encouraged him to take up the trumpet and form his first group, Chance, at the age of 14. 'I listened to everything and I still do,' he says. 'Prince is my favourite, but I also listen to Elton John, Bowie, Seal, The Beatles, The Rolling Stones, The Eagles, The Commodores. God, there are so many.'

Haddaway agrees that it is his diverse taste in music which gives his own so much character.

'I would say that my music has its roots in mid-70s pop and my voice is a combination of soul and 90s pop.' To this classic formula Haddaway has added the ever-popular standard European four to the floor beat and glorious double melodies. The combination has proved irresistible.

Ben Harper

Born October 28 1969, Harper was raised in the Inland Empire region of California (a semi-desert area 50 miles east of Los Angeles). As his interest in music grew, he delved into acoustic guitar and related instruments, especially dobro and Weissenborn, a hollow-necked lap slide guitar built by Herman Weissenborn during the mid-1920s to early 1930s. Yet Harper never matched the stereotypical idea of the reclusive young artist. In fact, much of his youth was spent skateboarding with his pals.

After signing with Virgin Records in 1993, Harper released his self-produced debut album, *Welcome To The Cruel World*, in July 1994. Enthusiastic reviews heralded its arrival. Declaring Harper 'young and gifted', *Rolling Stone* welcomed his 'vivid debut'. *Billboard* noted 'some of these songs have the ring of classics, lingering in the listener's mind long after they're gone. A laudable debut.'

Following warm praise from impressed fans and journalists, Harper toured through the U.S. and Europe – both as a headliner, and on the bill with an extremely diverse group of artists. During nearly two years of touring, his compelling performances have drawn rapt attention from all types of audiences.

'The reaction has been astounding, and let me tell you, a lot of these people had never seen an acoustic slide guitar live, ever. It was so foreign to many of them, and yet it was so well-received. Different cultures, different languages, different worlds almost – yet music provides that common ground. I didn't know how true that is until I went out on the road.'

Onstage and in the studio, Harper remains committed to exploring the language of music – although he shies away from describing it as acoustic music.

'Anyone who says they're playing acoustic but has a pickup in their instrument and is plugged into an amplifier, is *not* playing acoustic. That instrument has its own sound – different from acoustic, different from electric.'

He smiles and shakes his head in gentle resignation. 'Talking about music, you run the risk of sounding like a complete idiot. What more can you say about something that has already been stated in the best way you are able to say it?'

Hole

Rock band Hole began in Los Angeles in late 1989, and have since relocated to Seattle in order to take part in that city's exciting music scene. Drummer Patty Schemel used to play in some other bands in Seattle, one of which was called (for obscure religious reasons) Sybil. She joined Hole in mid-1992. Bass player Melissa Auf der Maur, a native of Canada and a damn fine crossword puzzler, signed on in 1994. Courtney Love, a renowned (in elite gourmet circles) pastry chef, and Eric Erlandson – a tall mysterious man with laughing eyes about whom little is known – are both original members.

In addition to writing and recording their long player *Live Through This* they played a week of dates that summer with Nine Inch Nails to get back to their goth roots. With those roots firmly in place, Hole embarked on a fall tour of North America where they headlined. While finishing up their tour the band learned that their album had gone gold in the U.S. There was much rejoicing!

The band then appeared on *Saturday Night Live*'s Christmas show when they exchanged gifts with host George Foreman. Patty takes the heavyweight championship belt that Foreman gave her everywhere she goes!

In 1995 the band decided they were tired of the cold winter and in January they went to Australia – where it was still summer – and played a whole bunch of dates. Next were a few dates in Japan where Eric became a hero to the Japanese for reasons that no one can explain. Hole returned to the States where they showed their soft and sensitive side by playing an acoustic show for the MTV *Unplugged* series. An old roommate of Courtney's, Hal Wilner, helped with the sound for the show.

Whitney Houston

Date of Birth: 9.8.64
Star Sign: Leo

Best Record Positions:

1985	'Saving All My Love For You'	No. 1	16 weeks
1987	'I Wanna Dance With Someone'	No. 1	16 weeks
1988	'One Moment In Time'	No. 1	12 weeks
1990	'I'm Your Baby Tonight'	No. 5	9 weeks
1992	'I Will Always Love You'	No. 1	23 weeks
1993	'I'm Every Woman'	No. 4	11 weeks
1993	'I Have Nothing'	No. 3	10 weeks

99

INXS

INXS originally formed in 1977 as The Farriss Brothers, since when the line-up has remained unchanged.

Straight out of high school, the entire band moved from their native Sydney to Perth where they wrote, rehearsed and, most importantly, began playing local hotels and pubs in mining towns. They played in places that, as somebody once noted, *Mad Max* territory look like a Japanese garden'. In 1979, they returned to Sydney where they renamed the band,

and made their live debut as INXS.

By the release of their first album in Australia in the fall of 1980, they were playing virtually seven nights a week. The following year they played no less than 300 gigs across Australia. Around the world, as in their homeland, it was through live performance that the band built their fanatical following.

In February 1983, they released their first U.S. Album, *Shabooh Shoobah*, featuring 'The One Thing', which made the Top 30 on the U.S. *Billboard* pop chart. In March, they began a marathon U.S. tour, appearing at the massive U.S. Festival in California. In 1984, the band released *The Swing*, debuting at No. 1 on the Australian charts. The single 'Original Sin', went to No. 1 in France and Argentina, underlining the band's growing international reputation.

In 1985, INXS played Live Aid in Australia, a performance that was beamed around the world. *The Swing* went double platinum in their homeland, ranking it as one of the top five albums in Australian history! The band also won an unprecedented number of Countdown Awards, Australia's equivalent of the Grammy.

By 1986, they had played over 1,500 live concerts around the world. That year, they also landed their first U.S. Top 5 single, 'What You Need', pulled from their first U.S. million seller, *Listen Like Thieves*, which had gone triple platinum in Australia.

In 1987 came *Kick*, which sold over four million copies in the United States alone and another five million worldwide! Four singles made the Top 10 on the US *Billboard* chart: 'Need You Tonight' (No. 1), 'Devil Inside' (No. 2), 'New Sensation' (No. 3), and 'Never Tear Us Apart' (No. 4). In addition, INXS earned a Grammy nomination, landed five MTV Video Music Awards and were awarded platinum certification of their long form home video, 'Kick – The Video Flick'. This was followed by a marathon 16-month global trek which well and truly kicked INXS into top gear.

In 1989, the members of INXS reconvened after some time off from the *Kick* hysteria, writing songs for their next album. The results were heard in late 1990, when they released *X*, an album that marked a major step forward. More musically challenging than *Kick*, *X* led off with a single, 'Suicide Blonde', featuring top American blues harpist, the great Charles Mussellwhite. It reached No. 9 on the *Billboard* chart, while the album sold nearly two million copies in the U.S. and a total of 3.5 million

INXS

worldwide. A triumphant year-long world tour followed. In July 1991, INXS reached a milestone in their 14–year odyssey when they headlined London's Wembley Stadium, performing in front of a 75,000 audience. As Tim Farriss comments, 'Wembley Stadium was like the biggest pub we ever played.' November 1991 saw the release of *Live Baby Live* and marked the band's first live album, compiled from the many band concerts over the years and including 16 songs recorded in 15 different cities around the world!

In 1992, INXS made history when they organised the biggest rock concert ever in Australian history, a benefit for AIDS and cardiac research and hospices. Taking place at Sydney's Centennial Park, the event drew more than 100,000 people, marking it as the biggest public gathering there since the 1901 celebration of Australia's federation!

As their record will attest, INXS have conquered the world – if not saved it!

Iron Maiden

Date of Birth:

Bruce Dickinson	7.8.58
Dave Murray	23.12.58
Clive Blurr	7.3.57
Steve Harris	12.3.57

Star Sign:

Bruce	Leo
Dave	Capricorn
Clive	Pisces
Steve	Pisces

Best Record Positions:

1988	'Can I Play With Madness'	No. 3	6 weeks
1988	'The Evil That Men Do'	No. 5	6 weeks
1990	'Holy Smoke'	No. 3	4 weeks
1991	'Bring Your Daughter... To The Slaughter'	No. 1	5 weeks
1992	'Be Quick or Dead'	No. 2	4 weeks
1993	'Fear Of The Dark'	No. 8	3 weeks
1993	'Hallowed Be Thy Name'	No. 9	3 weeks

Michael Jackson

Michael Jackson's story is the stuff of legends. It is a saga that began in America's heartland – Gary, Indiana, where Michael was born on August 29th 1958 to Joseph and Katherine Jackson, into a family of eight brothers and sisters. When papa Joe, himself a guitar player, noticed his sons' growing interest in music and performing, he devoted himself to the careful development of their natural talents. Through hard work and dedication, Michael, Marlon, Tito, Jermaine and Jackie became The Jackson 5.

The group began performing professionally in and around Gary in 1964 and later that year the siblings took their polished song-and-dance act to New York and Harlem's famed Apollo Theatre. The Jackson 5 turned the place out, winning first place in the Apollo's legendary amateur night talent show, where the audience reaction was (and still is) often brutal when a performance fails to meet the Apollo's high standards.

After years of relentless rehearsal and weekend gigs, the young group turned the corner. In 1969, led by the innate singing and performing ability of the prodigal 11-year-old Michael, the J-5 auditioned for Berry Gordy, founder of the Detroit-based Motown Records, then the most successful R&B label around. Captivated by what he saw and heard, Gordy signed the brothers immediately.

Thus began one of the most successful runs by a recording group in pop music history. Beginning in 1969, The Jackson 5 scored four consecutive No. 1 pop singles: 'I Want You Back', 'ABC', 'The Love You Save', and 'I'll Be There'. Not since the Beatles had any group enjoyed such an immediate and meteoric rise, a level of mass popularity capable of transcending all barriers of age and colour.

Motown soon began developing Michael's formidable talents as a solo artist. In the years 1971 to 1976, he scored with the singles 'Got To Be There', 'Rockin' Robin', 'I Wanna Be Where You Are' and 'Ben', the hit from the film of the same name. With his solo albums *Got To Be There*, *Ben*, *Music & Me*, *Forever Michael* and *The Best of Michael Jackson*, it was becoming increasingly clear that young Michael was not just an outstanding singer, but a true artist of potentially enduring impact.

Michael tended to these solo interests while fronting The Jackson 5, whose first three albums – *Diana Ross Presents The Jackson 5*, *ABC* and *Third Album*, all Top 5 best-sellers – were complemented by such hit singles as 'Never Can Say Goodbye', 'Mama's Pearl', 'Get It Together', 'Dancing Machine', and 'Forever Came Today'. Subsequent LPs included *Get It Together*, *Dancing Machine* and *Going Back To Indiana*. When The Jackson 5 weren't recording, they were headlining sell-out concert tours that took them around the world. The group's opening act was a then unknown band called The Commodores, led by a fellow named Lionel Richie!

After recording some 11 albums for Motown, The Jackson 5 left the label in 1976 to sign with the Epic subsidiary of CBS Records (now Sony Music). That same year, Motown released its *Jackson Five Anthology* greatest hits compilation, which underscored the fact that, by the time of its demise, the group had sold more than 100 million records worldwide.

Released in 1979, *Off The Wall* was Michael's first solo album as an adult; The album produced four hit singles: the No. 1 'Don't Stop Till You Get Enough', which also earned Michael his first solo Grammy Award for Best Male R&B Vocal Performance; the No. 1 'Rock With You'; 'She's Out Of My Life'; and 'Off The Wall'. The two No.1 singles sold more than one million copies each, and *Off The Wall* stayed on *Billboard*'s Top 100 album chart for 84 weeks (including eight months in the Top 10), selling more than five million copies in the U.S. and another three million worldwide!

Still doing double-duty as a member of The Jacksons, Michael led the group's 1980 album *Triumph* to platinum-status with the singles 'Lovely One', 'Heartbreak Hotel' and 'Can You Feel It'. The dynamic 'Heartbreak Hotel' in particular would introduce Michael's lyrical fixation with mystery, betrayal and romantic intrigue – all recurring themes in future Jackson compositions. The following year, 1981, The Jacksons embarked on one of their most successful tours ever, a 36-city trek that grossed $5.5 million and raised more than $100,000 for the Atlanta Children's Foundation during a benefit performance. Later that same year Epic released a double album set from the tour, *The Jacksons Live!*

For Michael Jackson, October 1982 commenced calmly enough, at least in the musical sense. After all, the first single from *Thriller*, his second Epic solo album, was 'The Girl Is Mine', a laidback mid-tempo duet performed and co-written by Michael and Paul McCartney. The single quickly sold a million copies, clearing the launch pad for *Thriller*.

Thriller arrived in the shops on December 1st, just in time for Christmas; by the year's end, it had sold more than one million copies. January 1983 saw the release of the album's second single, 'Billie Jean', which within three weeks had captured the No. 1 R&B slot and, in just over a month, topped the pop chart as well. *Thriller* conquered the No. 1 pop album slot in February 1983. The flames were fanned that May when, during a reunion of the original Jacksons line-up (including Jermaine) on the national televised 'Motown 25th Anniversary Special', Michael, alone in the white spotlight, performed 'Billie Jean'. This tour de force performance, featuring Jackson's now historic Moonwalk Dance, was seen by more than 50 million American viewers and millions more worldwide. Following Michael's dazzling performance, sales of *Thriller* went through the roof.

Thriller's next single, 'Wanna Be Startin' Somethin', went Top 5, followed by the Top 10 hits 'Human

Nature' and 'P.Y.T. (Pretty Young Thing)'. 'Say, Say, Say' – a duet performed and written by Michael and Paul McCartney from McCartney's album *Pipes Of Peace* – went to No. 1 in December 1983.
Thriller had already sold more than 10 million copies when in December 1983 the fabled 14-minute film 'Thriller' debuted on MTV. Today 'Thriller' is considered the most important clip in music video history, and not only for its state-of-the-art production. The film turned 'Thriller' into the album's record-breaking sixth Top 10 single, and propelled *Thriller* into the Guinness Book Of World Records as the best-selling album in history!! Not surprisingly *The Making Of Michael Jackson's Thriller*, became the largest selling music home video ever, with more than 900,000 units sold.

Michael's next career landmark occurred in January 1985, Michael Jackson and Lionel Richie teamed to compose 'We Are The World', an anthem of hope aimed at raising awareness in the battle against world hunger. Produced by Quincy Jones, the recording released in March 1985 featured more than 40 guest star artists performing as USA (United Support Artists) For Africa. Four million copies later – a portion of which profits went to the charity organisation USA for Africa to feed the continent's starving – 'We Are The World' became the best-selling single in history.

In August 1987 the single 'I Just Can't Stop Loving You', a duet between Michael Jackson and singer Siedah Garret, was released; its immediate acceptance at radio and retail quickly took the song to No. 1. On August 31, Michael's *Bad* album arrived in stores, with the largest advance orders for any album ever. That same day, CBS-TV aired the prime–time special 'Michael Jackson: The Magic Returns', which premiered Jackson's 17-minute 'Bad' short film, directed by Martin Scorsese (*Taxi Driver*, *Raging Bull*). It was Michaelmania all over again, as *Bad* became the first album in history to spin off five No. 1 pop singles ('Dirty Diana', 'Man In The Mirror', 'The Way You Make Me Feel', 'Bad' and 'I Just Can't Stop Loving You') and the second best-selling (non-soundtrack) album in history behind *Thriller*. The *Bad* tour – Michael's first ever as a solo artist – began in Japan and hit 127 dates in 15 countries, playing to nearly five million fans. By its conclusion, in Los Angeles in January 1989, the tour had set a world record gross of more than $125 million!

In April 1988, Michael proved that he would dominate

more than music charts when his autobiography *Moonwalker*, edited by Jacqueline Onassis, topped the best-seller lists in both the U.S. and U.K. Now firmly entrenched in the visual arts, Michael released the video film *Moonwalker*, a 94-minute fantasy of music, dance and special effects. Like everything else Jackson had touched, it too went to No. 1 on *Billboard*'s Video Sales chart, overtaking 1983's *The Making Of Michael Jackson's Thriller* as the largest selling music home video with over one million units sold. Remarkably, *Moonwalker* was displaced from the top slot by the May '89 video release *Michael Jackson . . . The Legend Continues*, which with a whopping 500,000 sales became the second all-time best-selling music video, after *Moonwalker*..

On September 5 1991, MTV changed its Video Vanguard Award to the Michael Jackson Video Vanguard Award in the star's honour. A month later, on November 11, 'Black or White' was released as the first single from *Dangerous*; it would hold the No. 1 pop position for seven weeks. True to Michael's groundbreaking spirit, the 'Black or White' short film featured a striking new visual effect called morphing. In November, the 11-minute 'Black or White' had its global television premiere.

Dangerous, fuelled by the No. 1 R&B singles 'Remember The Time' (No. 3) and 'In The Closet (No. 6) and the No. 3 R&B hit 'Jam', sold more than 17 million copies worldwide. The *Dangerous* tour dominated every country it flew to: in Japan alone, Michael played eight sold-out shows to more than 500,000 fans.

With the dawn of 1993, Michael and his music took over TV screens around the world. His shimmering January 31 half-time performance during Superbowl XXVII drew the single largest American viewing audience in television history. On February 10, his exclusive prime-time TV interview with Oprah Winfrey was viewed by 100 million people. On February 24, 1.2 billion viewers around the world tuned in to the 35th Grammy Awards to watch Michael's performance and his acceptance of the Living Legend Award.

Elton John

| Date of Birth: | | 25.3.47 |
| Star Sign: | | Aries |

Best Record Positions:

1972	'Rocket Man'	No. 2	13 weeks
1983	'I'm Still Standing'	No. 4	11 weeks
1984	'Sad Songs'	No. 7	12 weeks
1984	'Passengers'	No. 5	11 weeks
1985	'Nikita'	No. 3	13 weeks
1988	'Candle In The Wind'	No. 5	11 weeks
1990	'Sacrifice'	No. 1	15 weeks
1991	'Don't Let The Sun Go Down On Me'	No. 1	10 weeks
1993	'True Love'	No. 2	10 weeks
1994	'Don't Go Breaking My Heart'	No. 7	7 weeks

Lenny Kravitz

Some people dream in colour: others in black and white. Lenny Kravitz dreams in music. 'I was in Amsterdam,' he recalls, 'and it was three in the morning. I heard it all – the melody, words, everything. I woke up, ran into the bathroom and started singing into this little tape recorder. Then I cut it the next day in the studio.' He's talking about 'Don't Go Put a Bullet in Your Head', one of the more incendiary tracks off *Circus*. And while others among his 11 new songs were generated simply through hard work, intuitive experiment or a flash of inspiration, Lenny's fourth album indeed qualifies as his most explosive. It's a true music lover's dream: a dazzling carnival of rock and funk, ballads and barbed guitar.

The sonic charge of 'Rock 'n' Roll is Dead' detonates the record with, Kravitz says, 'a riff I came up with in a soundcheck in Japan'. The song attacks the 'giant corporate whitebread bubblegum machine that we're all a part of' and 'the clichéd rock 'n' roll lifestyle'. Countering the poseurs, Kravitz offers real emotion, genuine passion. The song delivers its message loud and clear: 'Be whoever you are: be the person who's inside you.'

From the out-of-nowhere blast of his 1989 debut *Let Love Rule* to the dark verve of *Mama Said* (1991) and the stylistic range of *Are You Gonna Go My Way* (1993), Lenny Kravitz has always been about self-expression. About communicating beyond all boundaries. The musician himself, half-Bohemian, half-Jewish, the son of NBC producer Sy Kravitz and actress Roxie Roker, was raised to recognise his limitations. During his boyhood, spent both on Manhattan's posh Upper East Side and the tough Brooklyn streets of Bedford-Stuyvesant, he was weaned on jazz (literally sitting on Duke Ellington's lap) and classical music (moving to LA, he sang with the prestigious California Boys Choir and The Metropolitan Opera, and recorded with Zubin Mehta). Add an early thirst for R&B, The Beatles, gospel, funk, reggae and Hendrix, and you have a musician impatient with anything that restricts the spirit.

No surprise, then, that Kravitz's inspiration derives from a place beyond all borders, a world beyond worlds. 'Every year I've been on the planet, I'm more sure that spirituality is real,' he says. Check the true soul power and gorgeous melodicism of 'God' and 'Today'. Catch the epic sweep of 'The Resurrection', a song whose grandeur recalls Lenny's classical training but whose drums are pure thunder.

Speaking of drums, *Circus* is its creator's most assertively rhythmic disc to date. 'Playing drums is how I have the most fun,' Lenny says, and his joy in commanding the kit is obvious in 'Beyond the 7th Sky' (my favourite drum sound on the record) and the unadulterated funk of 'Thin Ice' and 'Tunnel Vision' ('another soundcheck spin-off'). While guitarist Craig Ross assists on some cuts, Kravitz is nearly the exclusive instrumental force on *Circus*, alternating 10 or 12 guitars (but relying on his fave Les Paul) and crafting irresistibly tuneful bass-lines (pay heed to 'Magdalene' and 'Thin Ice'). In tune with longtime studio collaborator Henry Hirsch, Kravitz's trademark pre-digital recording technique achieves a sound as real as the songs are honest ('I think my records just keep getting rawer,' he says). Notice too the composer's gift for detail: the edgy wah-wah on the tale of a street bustler ('Thin Ice'), the ethereal multi-cracked vocals on 'God'.

Lenny Kravitz's singing is exultant, knowing, sharp – singing that comes straight from the soul.

Cyndi Lauper

Cyndi Lauper was born in Brooklyn, New York. She took up guitar at the age of 12, composing and playing in folk-based style through her teens while she attended several arts-oriented high schools. Cyndi joined her first semi-pro rock band in college, and paid her dues in the mid-70s as a vocalist with cover bands in the New York areas.

'I sang some Janis Joplin songs, and also Jefferson Airplane, Led Zeppelin, Bad Company . . . I tell ya, if I had to sing "White Rabbit" one more time, I was gonna die!' she remembers.

In 1987, Cyndi and multi-instrumentalist John Turi formed Blue Angel, co-writing the band's original material. Blue Angel released an eponymous album in 1980, but foundered on consumer and programmer indifference.

Cyndi Lauper signed with Portrait Records (a subsidiary of Epic Records) as a solo artist in the spring of 1983. Her debut album, *She's So Unusual*, was issued in January 1984 and went on to sell more than 4.5 million copies in the U.S. alone! It was the first debut album, and the first album by a solo artist, to spin off four Top 5 singles: 'Girls Just Want To Have Fun', 'All Through The Night', 'She Bop' and the No. 1 'Time After Time' (the latter co-written by

Cyndi and Rob Hyman of the Hooters). In 1984 Cyndi was voted *Rolling Stone*'s Best New Artist and Best Female Video Artist in the MTV Music Video Awards. She earned the Grammy Award for Best New Artist and two American Music Awards for Favourite Female Vocalist (Pop/Rock) and Favourite Female Vocalist Video (Pop/Rock).

In September 1986, Cyndi released her second Epic album *True Colors*, which she co-produced. The title track became a No. 1 pop smash and was nominated for a Grammy. Cyndi's subsequent world tour included a sold-out Paris concert, later preserved on the Sony video *Cyndi Lauper In Paris.*

In the summer of 1988, the singer co-starred with Jeff Goldblum and Peter Falk in the Columbia movie *Vibes*. The movie was not a commercial success, but Cyndi's vivacious screen presence and comedic talent were widely praised. Other film credits include *Off And Running* and *Life With Mikey*. In June 1988, the singer graduated (at last!) from Richmond Hill High School, when she was presented with an honorary diploma in a ceremony held at Queens College.

In October 1988, Cyndi travelled to the Soviet Union as one of a group of American songwriters collaborating with Soviet counterparts. Her third Epic album, *A Night To Remember*, was issued in April 1989. She wrote or co-wrote eight of the 11 tracks, and co-produced most of the album. The supporting cast included Eric Clapton, Bootsy Collins, Rockin' Dopsie, and Larry Blackmon and Nathan Leftenant of Cameo. The single 'I Drove All Night' was nominated for a Grammy Award.

In November 1991, Cyndi and actor David Thornton were married at Gramercy Park in Manhattan. Little Richard led the couple in the recitation of their non-traditional vows, and Patti LaBelle sang the wedding theme 'Come What May'.

Hat Full Of Stars, Cyndi's fourth Epic album, was issued in June 1993, co-produced by Cyndi with Junior Vasquez. She says, 'I wanted to make the album I always needed to make. I had to say the things I never could.'

In 1994, Cyndi appeared as a guest star on the hit television series *Mad About You*, for which she earned an Emmy Award nomination, and recently reprised her role of Mary Ann for which she is to receive a second Emmy nomination.

Multi-talented, this girl is guaranteed to have fun.

Annie Lennox

Annie Lennox

The Eurythmics' first album, *In The Garden*, was released in 1981 and drew upon the European electro-rhythms prevalent at the time. *In The Garden* paved the way for 1983's *Sweet Dreams (Are Made Of This)* which fused a mainstream sound with images more normally associated with the underground. The third album, *Touch*, included the singles 'Here Comes The Rain Again' and 'Right By Your Side'. Its success attracted the attention of film director Michael Radford, for whose adaptation of the George Orwell novel *1984* they contributed a highly idiosyncratic soundtrack.

1985's album, *Be Yourself Tonight*, heralded a move back to their soul and R&B roots, and included collaborations with Stevie Wonder, Aretha Franklin and Elvis Costello. *Revenge*, released in the summer of 1986, marked an abrupt change in direction. Their most rock-orientated album, it was supported by an 18-month world tour.

1987's critically acclaimed *Savage* album continued this process of diversification, gathering together an often bleak series of observations on sex and womanhood. *We Too Are One* was released in 1989, supported by the 66-date World Revival Tour. *Eurythmics Greatest Hits* album was released in 1991.

Altogether, the Eurythmics have sold in excess of 23 million albums worldwide, making Annie Lennox and Dave Stewart the most successful male-female pop duo of all time.

Annie's 1992 debut solo album, *Diva*, achieved quadruple platinum status in the U.K., with worldwide sales in excess of five million copies. The album spawned five hit singes: 'Why', 'Precious', 'Walking on Broken Glass', 'Cold' and 'Little Bird/Love Song For A Vampire'.

The success of *Diva* was crowned with two Brit Awards for Best Female Artist and Best Album. In the Grammy Awards, Annie was nominated for Best Female Artist and Best Album and won Best Longform Video. The 'Why' video won the best video category at the MTV Awards.

Stephen Lipson, the album's producer, was awarded with the Best Producer credit for *Diva* at the 1993 Music Week Awards. Other awards included Best Female Artist (*Rolling Stone*) and Europe's Most Successful Female Artist for 1992 (*Music & Media*).

As Annie says, '*Medusa* has risen from the need to do something different. To qualify that, from the early 80s I've been writing and co-writing songs and arrived at the stage where I just wanted to break that pattern for a while. Once the notion started I was inspired to follow it through.

Medusa sold over 4 million copies and included the singles 'No More I Love You's', 'Whiter Shade of Pale', 'Waiting In Vain' and 'Something So Right' (featuring Paul Simon). All chalking up massive around the globe sales.

Annie completed her first live dates in six years, headlining the Spot Festival in Gdansk, Poland in August 1995 and Central Park, New York in September plus a charity concert with Paul Simon and Pete Townshend at The Paramount, New York. Annie Lennox clearly carries on where the Eurythmics left off and I'm certain her mentor Dave Stewart will be delighted with her solo success.

Lightning Seeds

Perhaps what they said was right. Ian Broudie's last
two albums as the Lightning Seeds – 1990's
Cloudcuckooland and 1992's *Sense* – were hailed by
many as timeless portions of perfect pop. Dig them
out and stick them back on the stereo today and they
still sound every bit as fresh and instant as they did
before.

With *Jollification* Ian Broudie proved that his musical
vocabulary was still expanding. From the start the
buoyant mood and ambivalent nostalgia of album
opener 'Perfect' was complemented by the lively
melody, brisk edge and bitter-sweet sentiment of first
single 'Lucky You'. While the dry, gallows humour of
'Marvellous' is clothed in punchy, electro-pop garb,
elsewhere the strutting rhythm and insistent groove
of 'My Best Day' typify the infectious sparks sent
flying throughout the album.

It's a kind of apt that the man whose 1992 hit single
'The Life Of Riley' was adopted by BBCtv's *Match of
the Day* as the vibrant musical backdrop to their
'goals of the week' should be a passionate advocate
of the beautiful game. It's possible to sense the

parallel passion Broudie feels for music. 'The idea that you can make this thing, this piece of music that can relate to people through the airwaves, is fantastic,' he enthuses. 'You're making these little pieces of time, and years later they will still be there.'

As a prolific songwriter, whose Lightning Seeds chart hits also include 1992's 'Sense' and 'Pure' from 1989, as well as a sought-after record producer for bands from Echo & The Bunnymen to Dodgy and Sleeper, he has been round a little while. But somehow he's never lost his wide-eyed enthusiasm for making music. 'So much of the fun when you're recording a song is that there are all these possibilities and in the end it could be absolutely anything,' he says.

Broudie approached *Jollification* with the accent on spontaneity, writing the songs as he went along. 'I always had the end in sight,' he says. 'I knew the melodies and the structure vaguely, but there was nothing beyond that.' He also decided on a change in technical approach, choosing to shape the songs around the use of loops much more than he had before. 'I thought it would be challenging to approach it in that way. To use loops and really try to force them into the structures. I don't think anyone's ever really done that with songs and still achieved freshness and atmosphere.'

Friend and fellow songwriter Terry Hall is another with a reputation for mixing the barbed with the beautiful. As with 'Sense', the pair collaborated again for the album, this time on 'Lucky You'. *Jollification* found Broudie teaming up again with Ian McNab on the suburban vignette 'Feeling Lazy' and, for the first time, with fellow songwriter Alison Moyet on 'My Best Day'.

With *Jollification*, Broudie was very keen to get out and play the songs live for the first time. He regrets not having the confidence to do it before. 'I would really have loved to have played the songs on the other albums on stage afterwards,' he says. 'I think that's where they really take on a new life.' Lightning Seeds played London's Borderline to massive critical acclaim: 'one of the seventh wonders of the modern pop Valhall' (*Melody Maker*), 'pure pop blinking in the headlights' (*The Times*), with everyone wondering why they'd never played before.

Jollification was released in September 1994 to superb critical acclaim: 'exquisitely realised modern pop' (*Details*); 'a marvellous, magical pop record'

(*Melody Maker*); 'if there was an award for Perfect English Fey Pop band, the Lightning Seeds would win, no contest – a crystalline watermark' (*Q*). The singles 'Change' and 'Marvellous' went Top 30 with 'Change' peaking at No. 13. Lightning Seeds continued touring throughout Britain in January, headlining the LA2, followed by a European tour co-headlining with Dodgy. And public demand ensured that the band were again out on tour during May, this time playing sold out shows to 2,000 people a time. 'Lightning Seeds bounce with triumphancy; each song is a celebration of romantic optimism and the vagaries of passion . . . Even God is touched by the hand of Lightning Seeds' (*Melody Maker*).

Now would probably be a good time to catch Lightning Seeds live, because Broudie already has his thoughts about album four. 'With the addition of *Jollification* these three LPs fit together well,' he says. 'The next one will be very different.'

Louise

As most people will already be aware, Louise was
elevated to international stardom during her three
years as part of the all-girl singing sensation Eternal.
The group had unprecedented success, selling over
three million copies of their first album, *Always &
Forever*. Singles success was no less spectacular.
Their first release, 'Stay', reached No. 4 and was
swiftly followed by five other Top 10 hits, a string
of awards and bags of fan mail. Eternal were unique
not only for their top quality pop tunes, strong vocal
performances and good looks but for their ability to
attract without alienating girls of their own age. Louise
now takes this distinction and flair into her solo
career.

When Louise's past achievements are considered she
was perhaps always destined for solo success. Born
4 November 1974 in South London, she attended
regular school until she was 11 when her
headmistress suggested that her parents guide her
towards stage school. Louise was, to proffer an

understatement, not at all keen. Nevertheless, within three months she had endured an entrance audition and on her birthday received news of her acceptance to the Italia Conti Stage School. It might have been the worst birthday present imaginable to her but it was the start of something big.

Some five years later Louise met Denis Ingoldsby who in turn introduced her to Easther and Vernie Bennett. She then brought along Kelle Bryan, a friend from Italia Conti, and Eternal was born and the rest, as they say, in the well-worn pop vernacular, is history.

When Louise left Eternal she had no idea what her next move might be but within hours of announcing her resignation, EMI had made a firm offer on a solo deal. And here she is. She may be moving on but she's still got her feet planted firmly on the ground. 'I've just grown a bit older now and my career reflects that. The one thing I'm sure of is that I don't want to sell out to my existing fans. My music and my image have moved on but I'll never be something I'm not. I'm just the same, but a bit more grown up. I look forward now to making my own decisions and even if they turn out to be the wrong decisions at least I'm learning.'

Apart from producing exquisite pop music, 'growing up' also entails living her life as a Young Independent Female, an unabashed 90s girl characterised by living alone and making bad shopping decisions like the time she spent £160 on a pair of super-trendy American trainers only to return to Britain to find they were on special offer at £13.99 in London. 'I'm a girlie and I'm not ashamed of it!' she says. 'I like going for picnics and crying at films – especially *About Last Night* with Demi Moore.'

Film is a big passion. 'I'm still very interested in acting. At the moment I'm watching a lot of English films but I'd have killed to play Whitney Houston's part in *The Bodyguard*.' Any other ambitions? 'Just to concentrate on my singing career and to cut loose a little. I like Prince because he's eccentric. I've been level-headed far too long. It's time to enjoy myself and let go.'

I don't think she's happy to settle for just a successful recording career nor good friends either. Simply eternally successful.

M People

The last three years have witnessed M People's meteoric rise from 'dance act' to 'pop band' to . . . 'household name'.

Their debut album on deConstruction Records, *Northern Soul* became one of the most exceptional dance albums of 1992, selling in excess of 100,000 (gold). The follow-up, *Elegant Slumming*, joined the ranks of classic home listening albums whilst still retaining the support of the band's club fan-base and went on to achieve double-platinum status.

1994 saw the release of their third album, *Bizarre Fruit*, which achieved platinum status inside a month whilst *Elegant Slumming* still held a Top 40 chart position!

The single 'Open Your Heart' released from that album reached No. 9 in the U.K. charts, and a lot of credit must go to Heather Small's unique vocal delivery and presence.

Their awards lay testimony to their popularity.

1993   Best Album of the year and Best Band of the Year voted by *M8* magazine readers

1994   Best Dance Act at the International Dance Awards

1994   Mercury Music Album of the Year Award for *Elegant Slumming*

1994   Short-listed for the Best Production award for the *Q* Magazine Awards

1994   Best British Act at the Brit Awards

1995   Best British Dance Act at the Brit Awards

1995   Dance Act of the Year at the International Dance Awards

1995   Best Dance Group and Best Overall Dance Act at the Miami Winter Conference

Madonna

Date of Birth:	16.8.58
Star Sign:	Leo

Best Record Positions:

1985	'Into The Groove'	No. 1	14 weeks
1986	'Papa Don't Preach'	No. 1	14 weeks
1986	'True Blue'	No. 1	15 weeks
1987	'La Isla Bonita'	No. 1	11 weeks
1987	'Who's That Girl'	No. 1	10 weeks
1989	'Like A Prayer'	No. 1	12 weeks
1990	'Vogue'	No. 1	14 weeks

Manic Street Preachers

Formed in the claustrophobic, closed-down mining town of Blackwood, South Wales, sometime in the late 1980s, Manic Street Preachers consists of cousins James Dean Bradfield (vocals/lead guitar) and Sean Moore (drums), who grew up in the same house, and their school friends Nicky Wire (bass) and Richey James (guitar).

Desperate to make an impression on a Manchester-dominated music scene, the group blended situationist slogans, glam homo-eroticism and fury for real rock 'n' roll and were soon hijacking the music press, citing the unlikely combination of Public Enemy and Guns 'N' Roses as the only current day musical heroes to aspire to. Manics interviews showed a focused intelligence rarely witnessed among their lazy contemporaries. They had an intense desire to be real stars and shunned the grey British indie scene. Their blend of cheap make-up and tacky Miss

Selfridge blouses put dressing up back on new bands agenda's!! Two singles – 'Motown Junk' and 'You Love Us' – released on the Heavenly label led to the band signing a worldwide deal with Columbia Records in the summer of 1991.

Always pledging to issue a debut double album, the band released *Generation Terrorists* in February 1992. It yielded six Top 40 singles – 'Stay Beautiful', 'Love's Sweet Exile', 'You Love Us', 'Slash 'n' Burn', 'Motorcycle Emptiness' and 'Little Baby Nothing'. The band enjoyed their biggest hit to date in September when they released a charity version of 'Theme From Mash'.

The Manics toured incessantly and at the end of '92 played a sell-out tour of Japan, where *Generation Terrorists* sold over 50,000 copies, a feat rarely achieved in recent years by British rock bands. The Manics have proved unique in that they have crossed over from the *NME* to *Kerrang*, from *Smash Hits* to *The Times*.

I won't preach to the converted as they are obviously up your street.

Manic Street Preachers released their second Columbia album – *Gold Against The Soul* – at the end of June. The ten-track record was produced by 21-year-old Dave Eringa who worked on the Manics early Heavenly singles. It captured the raw unpredictability that has made the Manics such an uptight live act and saw the Manic Street Preachers become a true classic British rock 'n' roll band for the 90s and spawned four Top 30 hits, 'From Despair To Where', 'La Tristesse Durera', 'Roses In The Hospital' and 'Life Becoming A Landslide'.

The group triumphed at the Phoenix 93, had a riot of an appearance at Swansea Heineken Festival in August and supported Bon Jovi at their two Milton Keynes dates in September. After a second sell-out tour of Japan in October, the Manics played their biggest tour to date including a sell-out at London's Brixton Academy.

The group entered the studio in early '94 to start work on their third album, *The Holy Bible*, interrupted only by a one-off show at The Grand in Clapham with the Pogues, where the Manics were joined on stage by Bernard Butler from Suede, in aid of the Imperial Cancer Research Fund.

After moving over to Epic Records, a brand new double A-sided single 'Faster/'PCP' was released in June 1994 to fantastic critical acclaim (single of the week/month in *NME* and *Select* respectively), and was the band's 12th consecutive Top 40 hit. The Manics played two legendary shows in Bangkok where they were the first 'alternative' group to play and received platinum discs for record sales in Thailand. MSP returned to play in front of 100,000 people at the Carnival against the Nazis in London's Brockwell Park and hijacked the Glastonbury Festival with a triumphant performance.

A new single 'Revol' was released on 1 August, and *The Holy Bible* the following month. The group appeared at the 94 Reading Festival and toured the UK throughout October.

George Michael

Date of Birth: **25.6.63**
Star Sign: **Gemini**

Best Record Positions:

1984	'Careless Whisper'	No. 1	17 weeks
1986	'A Different Corner'	No. 1	10 weeks
1987	'Faith'	No. 2	12 weeks
1991	'Don't Let The Sun Go Down On Me'	No. 1	10 weeks
1992	'Too Funky'	No. 4	9 weeks
1993	'Five Live' EP	No. 1	11 weeks

Kylie Minogue

Kylie signed to PWL in 1987 and her first album, *Kylie*, produced by Stock, Aitken and Waterman, spawned the No. 1 dance-floor anthem 'I Should Be So Lucky'. Four subsequent singles from the album were released; one graced the No. 1 position, the others climbed to No. 2. With the release of her duet with Jason Donovan, 'Especially For You', in November 1988, Kylie became the first female artist to have her first five singles all go 'silver' in the UK.

At the end of the year, her first video collection was released, *Kylie Minogue – the videos*. It debuted at No. 1. In 1989, Kylie's first feature film, *The Delinquents* was released. She played the female lead – Lola Lovell – in the 50s-based teenage love story. Whilst this was her feature film debut, Kylie began acting aged 11, appearing in the Australian shows *Skyways* and *The Sullivans*. In 1986, she landed the role of Charlene in *Neighbours*. She has been honoured with 9 Logies – the Australian TV industry awards.

In 1989, Kylie released the album *Enjoy Yourself*. The first single, 'Hand On Your Heart', reached No. 1. Three additional Top 5 singles followed, including the No. 1 'Tears On My Pillow' from *The Delinquents*. At the end of the year she collaborated with other pop luminaries such as Wet Wet Wet and Lisa Stansfield to record Band Aid II's 'Do They Know It's Christmas'. This No. 1 recording raised money for the Ethiopian crisis.

On New Year's Eve 1989, Clive James presented Kylie with the Woman Of The Decade award. In 1990 Kylie toured Australia, and then the U.K. to coincide with the release of 'Better The Devil You Know' from the *Rhythm Of Love* album.

Kylie's tour then proceeded to the Far East.

By now, Kylie had set the precedent of being the first artist to have her first 13 singles all reach the Top 10!

The *Rhythm Of Love* album featured collaborations with SAW, Michael Jay and Stephen Bray. Kylie co-wrote four of the tracks. In June 1991 she began work on her fourth album *Let's Get To It*. Kylie co-wrote six tracks including the Keith Washington duet 'If You Were With Me Now'. Her No. 1 *Greatest Hits* album was released in August 1992 featuring the new hit singles 'Celebration' and 'What Kind Of Fool'.

In April 1993, Kylie signed to Deconstruction and in 1994 appeared with Jean-Claude Van Damme and Raul Julia in the film *Streetfighter*, based on the multi-million dollar video game.

Kylie Minogue
Discography
Singles

'I Should Be So Lucky'	29/12/87	No. 1
'Got To Be Certain'	02/05/88	No. 2
'The Loco-Motion'	25/07/88	No. 2

'Je Ne Sais Pas Pourquoi	17/10/88	No. 2
'Especially For You'	28/11/88	No. 1
'Hand On Your Heart'	24/04/89	No. 1
'Wouldn't Change A Thing'	24/07/89	No. 2
'Never Too Late'	23/10/89	No. 4
'Tears On My Pillow'	08/01/90	No. 1
'Better The Devil You Know'	30/04/90	No. 2
'Step Back In Time'	22/10/90	No. 4
'What Do I Have To Do'	21/01/91	No. 6
'Shocked'	20/05/91	No. 6
'Word Is Out'	28/08/91	No. 14
'If You Were With Me Now'	21/10/91	No. 4
'Give Me Just A Little More Time'	13/01/92	No. 2
'Finer Feelings'	13/04/92	No. 11
'What Kind Of Fool'	10/08/92	No. 14
'Celebration'	16/11/92	No. 11

Albums

Kylie	04/07/88	No. 1
Enjoy Yourself	09/10/89	No. 1
Rhythm Of Love	12/11/90	No. 9
Let's Get To It	14/10/91	No. 15
Greatest Hits	24/08/92	No. 1

Sinead O'Connor

Sinead O'Connor moved to London in 1985, after
signing to Ensign Records, where she both wrote and
produced her first album *The Lion and the Cobra*
which was released to great critical acclaim in 1987.
She followed this album with tours of the U.K., U.S.A.
and Europe in 1988.

Sinead recorded her second album in London
during 1989. *I Do Not Want What I Haven't Got*
was released in the U.K. in March 1990, and went
straight into the album chart at No. 1. The first
single from that album was released in January
1990, 'Nothing Compares 2 U', a cover of a song
written by Prince which she first heard about three
years previously on an album by Minneapolis group
The Family. The single went on to be No. 1 in the
U.K., Ireland, The States, Germany, Holland, Italy –

17 countries in all! In September 1990, Sinead was awarded three MTV Music Awards in the U.S.A., including Best Video of the Year.

1991 saw Sinead living in Los Angeles having stayed on after the MTV awards, at which she won Best Single and Best Female Singer. In April, she returned to England to live and in May she released the single 'My Special Child', all the proceeds going to the Kurdish Refugee Appeal. She also played live that May at the Hague for the Kurdish Refugee Concert. In October of that year she went to Yorkshire for the filming of her part as Emily Bronte, the narrator in the film *Wuthering Heights*. Christmas saw Sinead in the Malcolm MacLaren-directed TV film *The Ghosts Of Oxford Street* where she sang the carol 'Silent Night', released as a single that December.

1992 saw Sinead spending April and May in New York at the National Edison Studios, with an orchestra of 47 musicians, recording her third album *Am I Not Your Girl?* The album, produced by Phil Ramone and Sinead herself, consisted of cover versions of classic songs that Sinead loved and wanted to sing. The first single, 'Success Has Made A Failure Of Our Home', was released in September and the album followed later that month when a BBC2 special about the making of the album was shown in the U.K.

In October, there was controversy in the U.S.A. after Sinead tore up a picture of the Pope on the *Saturday Night Live* TV programme, followed by Sinead's appearance at the Bob Dylan Tribute concert at Madison Square Gardens where there was a fierce audience reaction; she went on to perform 'War' by Bob Marley. In November Sinead donated her house in LA to raise money for the Red Cross Somalia appeal fund, and later that month she appeared at the Royal Festival Hall in the Amnesty International Concert for Human Rights. November also saw 'Don't Cry For Me Argentina' released as the last single from the album *Am I Not Your Girl?* In December, Sinead went to Dublin to record 'Be Still' for the 'Peace Together' project.

In March 1993 Sinead sang 'Make Me A Channel Of Your Peace' unaccompanied at the Dublin Peace Rally. She took up residence in Dublin and enrolled for singing lessons at the Parnell School of Music! In the summer, she made various guest appearances on the Peter Gabriel World Tour. In November she returned to Dublin to record 'You Made Me The Thief Of Your Heart', the closing music for the film about the Guildford Four *In The Name Of The Father*. The

song was released in February 1994 as a single.
In January 1994 she recorded the opening song for
Oh Mary This London, a new film for BBC Screen 2
directed by Suri Krishnamma and written by Shane
Connaughton (*My Left Foot*).

Sinead continued to write and compose her own
songs and in March she went into Westland Studios
in Dublin and recorded her fourth album, *Universal
Mother*, which was released in the U.K. in September.
Sinead produced *Universal Mother* herself with Tim
Simenon (Bomb The Bass), John Reynolds (drummer
with Jah Wobble) and Phil Coulte. The album
contained ten new songs written by Sinead and
two covers.

Oasis

The very first time Oasis played together they promised they were going to be the best, that they'd never settle for the dull thud of mediocrity. And then th~y set about proving it. Right from the off, they resisted the security of the obvious, of doing things the way they were supposed to. They neYer sent a demo to a record company, knew that supreme self-confidence and a host of classic songs would be enough to direct destiny their way. When Creation Records supremo Alan McGee saw them at a club gig in Glasgow they had no manager, no agent, and no money. Just greatness. Alan signed them on the spot, ensuring an unsuspecting world was about to be blown away.

In April 1994, Oasis released their debut single, 'Supersonic', an elegantly noisy pop celebration. By now their live shows were being talked of as something very special and they'd built an extensive, committed fan base. A trio of classic singles, 'Shakermaker', 'Live Forever' and 'Cigarettes and Alcohol' endorsed Oasis' searingly assured power as their increasingly growing audience began to wonder what they ever did without them. More live shows followed, including a triumphant New York debut and promoters soon not used to the band breaking all records, exceeding even the wildest expectations. With the release of their debut album, 'Definitely Maybe', it was time to rewrite the record books once again. That album was the fastest selling debut in British history

Pet Shop Boys

Date of Birth:

Neil Tennant	**10.7.54**
Chris Lowe	**14.10.59**

Star Sign:

Neil	**Cancer**
Chris	**Libra**

Best Record Positions:

1985	'West End Girls'	No. 1	15 weeks
1987	'It's A Sin'	No. 1	11 weeks
1987	'Always On My Mind'	No. 1	11 weeks
1988	'Heart'	No. 1	8 weeks
1988	'Left To My Own Devices'	No. 4	8 weeks
1990	'So Hard'	No. 4	6 weeks
1993	'Go West'	No. 2	9 weeks
1994	'Absolutely Fabulous'	No. 6	7 weeks

Prince

Date of Birth:	7.6.58
Star Sign:	Gemini

Best Record Positions:

1986	'Kiss'	No. 6	9 weeks
1989	'Batdance'	No. 2	12 weeks
1990	'Thieves In The Temple'	No. 7	6 weeks
1984	'When Doves Cry'	No. 4	15 weeks
1984	'Purple Rain'	No. 8	9 weeks
1985	'1999/ Little Red Corvette'	No. 2	10 weeks
1989	'Batdance'	No. 2	12 weeks
1992	'Sexy Me/Strollin''	No. 4	7 weeks
1993	'Controversy'	No. 5	5 weeks
1994	'The Most Beautiful Girl In The World'	No. 1	12 weeks

PJ & Duncan

Declan Joseph Oliver Donnelly was born on September 25 1975 on the west side of Newcastle-upon-Tyne. His Irish folks raised young Dec and his three older brothers and three older sisters as strict Catholics. They also introduced the youngsters to the delights of Irish dancing, a skill he soon mastered and for which he won stacks of gleaming trophies. Declan's other great passion was – and still is – football, so you can imagine how chuffed he was when his childhood footie idol, Kevin Keegan, became manager of his beloved team newcastle United.

Dec's first taste of showbusiness came when he was 13 and auditioned for the part in a Newcastle based children's series 'Byker Grove', which was all about the lives, loves, trials and tribulations of a group of kids at a local youth club. He won the role of Duncan, a major heart-throb and one of the teen drama's central characters. 'Byker' proved a huge success and a second series was commissioned a year later, which was when Declan first met his partner in crime, Anthony McPartlin, who was introduced as Duncan's best mate PJ.

Antony David McPartlin was born in Newcastle on November 18 1975. He's the eldest of three children and still lives at home with his parents and sisters. Like Dec, Ant's a massive Newcastle United fan and shares his passion for screaming along with thousands of other footie fans on the terraces of the 'Toon' (the Geordie term for Newcastle). Ant doesn't Irish dance, but musically, you name it and he'll give it a listen.

Ant joined 'Byker Grove' playing laddish PJ, whose strongest storyline involved him being blinded in a freak paintballing accident. Ant spent time with the Royal Institute for the Blind, researching his role and his resulting emotional scenes received widespread acclaim. Shortly afterwards PJ was written out of the series, allowing him and Dec, who left at the end of the 1993 run, to spend more time pursuing their own main interest – music.

As part of the 1993 Byker storylines, characters PJ & Duncan set up a band called Grove Matrix and attempted to make it in the music biz. Their song, 'Tonight I'm Free' (written by Let Loose especially for the series), caused such a sensation among the show's 7 million views who, by this time were also avid Ant & Dec fans, that the guys were signed to Telstar Records, who, due to public demand, released the track.

Although 'Tonight I'm Free' wasn't a huge hit, it nonetheless provided the perfect springboard for Ant & Dec who smoothly made the transition from TV heart-throbs to pop heart-throbs. using their natural talent for larking and pranking about and adopting the familiar household names of their former TV personas, the duo stormed into the UK Top 40 with their unique brand of humorous rap and pop. 'Let's Get Ready To Rhumble' was the summer smash of 1994, reaching Number 9, while 'If I Give You My Number' went on to make it to Number 15 and their seasonal ballad, 'Eternal Love' not only galloped to Number 12 in the UK Chart, but was the top of the pile for 5 consecutive weeks in Singapore. But that's just for starters!

PJ & Duncan's debut album, 'Psyche' received rave reviews in all the pop press and earned the twosome a platinum disc, selling over 400,000 copies in the UK alone. 'Psyche' was followed by the major success of Ant & Dec's longform home-made video, 'Whose Video Is It Anyway?' which reached a staggering Number 2 in the UK video chart. 1994 was rounded off on an equally high note when PJ & Duncan AKA, deservedly, won the Smash Hits/Radio 1 Best New Act of '94 Award at the Smash Hits Poll Winner's Party.

1995 kicked off with a nomination as Best Newcomer in the prestigious Brit Awards and another UK To 20 hit in the shape of 'Our Radio Rocks'. Then came the boy's biggest achievement to date – their very own eight-part BBC1 TV series. The Ant & Dec Show capitalised on the guys' ability to make a joke about absolutely anything and even send themselves up, featuring light hearted self written sketches, a spoof soap opera and a posse of showbiz guests including Dani Behr, Andi Peters, Russell Grant, and Baywatch's Jaason Simmons. We've been described as a cross between Vic Reeves and Bob Mortimer and Zig & Zag, which I think is a very big compliment' grins Ant. 'I was dead chuffed at that, me' laughs Declan 'although we get most of our inspiration from Bert and Ernie off Sesame Street'.

Pulp

Pulp or, as they were originally called, Arabacus Pulp (yes after the coffee bean), were formed in 1981 whilst Jarvis Cocker was still at school in Sheffield. Their first gigs were performed during their lunch hour in the canteen where they charged their peers a nominal fee for the pleasure/pain of watching their class mates perform. Whilst still there they became sufficiently accomplished and bizarrely interesting to record their first Peel Session. And then . . . well, then frankly there followed a few years of patient waiting during which time they managed intermittent record releases and Jarvis fell/jumped out of a window in order to impress a girlfriend and ended up in a wheelchair for over a year for his trouble! They recorded their first album 'It' in 1983 and then signed to Fire Records and recorded 'Freaks' in a week in 1986 for £600. During this period they had an allegedly disastrous relationship with Fire Records, which accounted for a long, long wait for their 3rd album 'Separations' which wasn't released by Fire until after they had signed to Island Records. During this seemingly disappointing period of time Jarvis and Steve moved to London whilst the others stayed in Sheffield. Jarvis went to St martin's to study film and Steve did a similar course at the RCA.

Pulp entered a state of semi-hibernation, meeting on a roughly bi-monthly basis and playing the (very) occasional gig, they maintained a nominal existence, little knowing that true recognition was just around the corner. Ironically, it was just as Pulp stopped really trying that the world took notice. Although Fire wouldn't release 'Separations' they did however unexpectedly release the track 'My Legendary Girlfriend' as a single in the spring of 1991. Suddenly, Pulp's idiosyncratic, dilettantish English pop was snugly 'in' with a year. In 1992 after having released themselves from Fire, Pulp released three singles on the Gift label: 'Razzmatazz', 'O.U.' and 'Babies'. Shortly after, Pulp were signed by Island Records who released 'PulpIntro. The Gift Records' which was intended as both a mid-priced introduction to, and as a time capsule of, the band's recent glittering past.

Pulp have since released a series of singles on Island and their first album on a major 'His 'N' Hers' which was nominated for the Mercury Music Prize, narrowly missing the coveted award by one vote! Since then, Jarvis has been seen presenting Top Of The Pops as well as appearing on it, being the star guest on Pop Quiz. Pulp also appeared at Glastonbury slotting in for Saturday night headliners. The previous year they had played a mid-afternoon slot on the NME stage. Much to their credit they pulled off a fantastic show. The band camped backstage for the entire weekend in two tents, which were not covered in gold lamé as Jarvis told the crowd, but became fondly termed as the Pulp camp.

Pulp do not merely produce records, they also make films. Both Steve and Jarvis have made videos for the Aphex Twin (which won an award at Soundcity) and the Tindersticks as well as their own videos for Pulp. Steve produced 'Carrera' in 1994 which was screened on Channel 4. Both Steve and Jarvis made a short documentary which was subsequently shown on Channel 4 – 'Do You Remember The First Time?'. Named after one of their songs the documentary was, well the title says it all about losing one's virginity! Various celebrities were interviewed about that rather delicate subject. Amongst those who faced a little probing from Jarvis were comedian Jo Brand, Justine Frischman from Elastica, the ever specials Terry Hall, designer Pam Hogg, both Vic Reeves and Bob Mortimer, John Peel, the man who said 'tubular bells!' – Vivient Stanshall and the actress Alison Steadman. All fairness was restored to he proceedings by Jarvis revealing the shabby details of his own deflowering!

And just to prove how multi-media and faceted this band truly are Jarvis designed a pair of shoes for the Brian Eno War Child fund raising auction in which Jarvis' shoes were sold (alongside Bryan Ferry's design for a Sellotape dress and David Bowie's design for a bandage and blood outfit) for the mere trifling figure of £5,100.

Pulp then played a Christmas Show at the Brixton Academy and not as they had hoped at the Palladium following the previous year's show at Drury Lane. Unfortunately Pulp are no longer permitted to perform at any London Theatres due to the crowd enjoying themselves too much at Drury Lane causing the ceiling to crack.

Pulp then released the highly acclaimed album 'Different Class' in October 1995, attaining the No. 1 spot the week of release and achieving platinum status after just ten days.

Rednex

Once upon this planet, in a century most corrupt,
a big-time Swedish producer, Pat Reniz, wanted to
change and challenge our perceptions of dance
music. He packed his holdall and his inhibitions and
set out on a journey most profound in search of the
Holy Grail.

His instincts led him to the isolated backwater village
of Brunkeflo City, in the state of Idaho, U.S.A. Here
he was invited to the regular Brunkeflo Barn Dance.
Music was provided by a five-piece band. Mary Joe
and Ken Tacky on vocals, Ken also on the banjo,
violins played by Billie Ray and Bobby Sue and Billy
Bob Stiff on the drums. The crowd's reaction to the
band was unforgettable, almost a frenzied eruption.
These talented hillbillies from the Rocky Mountain
prairies had brought Pat from a distant civilisation
into the next decade of dance music. Pat named the
band Rednex because of their sun-burnt necks from
working in the fields and brought them back to his
hometown of Sweden to produce their debut album

Sex and Violins on Internal Affairs. 'Cotton Eye Joe' was the first single to be released from the album. It reached No. 1 in nine European countries including the U.K., starting a new wave in dance music and causing a whirlwind on our dance-floors nationwide. Just how big are the Rednex?

Quite simply they are one of the most successful acts in Europe, and the world, today. 'Rednex Fever' that started with 'Cotton Eye Joe' last summer has snowballed into one of the most phenomenal success stories of the decade. Almost every week they set a new sales record somewhere in the world. Here are just a few:

- Worldwide total sales of nearly 7 million units.
- Biggest-selling single in Germany for over 10 years with sales of 'Cotton Eye Joe' mounting to 1.5 million. In Denmark it is the biggest-selling single ever!
- 'Cotton Eye Joe' sold over 3.5 million units worldwide and has amassed a total of 1 triple platinum, 2 double platinum, 4 platinum and 6 gold awards.
- The album *Sex and Violins* has sold 1.5 million units worldwide with 3 platinum and 8 gold awards.
- All three singles made Top 5 on the *Music & Media* Pan-European Hot 100. At one point 'Cotton Eye Joe' and 'Old Pop In An Oak' were at No. 1 and 4 respectively.
- In Sweden they outsell Take That by 2 to 1.
- Rednex have been continuously in the German Top 40 singles chart since last October, including a total of 16 weeks at No. 1
- On a worldwide scale, *Sex and Violins* is platinum in New Zealand and Canada and gold in Japan. They are big in countries as diverse as Poland, Brazil, Hungary, Latvia, Lebanon and India – in fact their album went to No. 1 in the latter two!

Robson and Jerome

Riding on the back of their Soldier Soldier popularity, Robson and Jerome's debut single 'Unchained Melody/White Cliffs Of Dover' entered the charts at No. 1 on the week of release, becoming the fastest-selling non-charity single ever! It stayed there for seven weeks keeping the likes of U2 and Michael Jackson off the top slot. As I write, the single has sold almost 2 million copies, making it the biggest-selling single of 1995! Now it's 'I Believe/Up On The Roof' which is again taking the charts by storm. As the actors who play Dave Tucker and Sgt Paddy Garvey in the hit series Soldier Soldier, the due originally performed their version of 'Unchained Melody' on television. Immediately viewers besieged records shops hoping to buy the record! But no matter how popular an actor is, unless they have that 'certain something' the fickle world of pop will not tolerate an attempt on the charts.

Robson and Jerome have clearly passed that acid test. Their album appropriately titled Robson and Jerome, which includes their renditions of such classics as 'The Sun Ain't Gonna Shine Anymore', 'Amazing Grace', 'Daydream Believer' and 'Danny

Boy', has generated massive sales and chart-topping positions.
Stand to attention and watch Robson and Jerome climb the ranks now they have won their stripes!

Swooners to Crooners!
Soldier Soldier heartthrobs Jerome Flynn and Robson Green are to play a Bing Crosby and Bob Hope-style duo in an ITV comedy.
Clapper and Trap is their own idea based on the 1940s Big Bandera and is bound to inspire a crop of new smash hits which will carry them along their 'road to further success'.

Mike Scott

Mike Scott

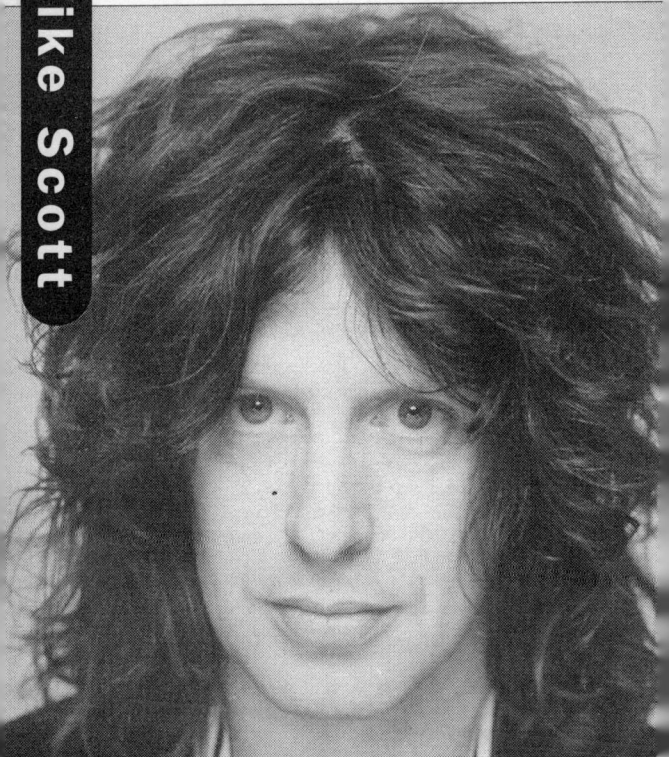

The evolution of Mike Scott's musical life – from wide-eyed, teenage rocker to enthralling story-spinner – is as rich and as unpredictable as any adventure quest. His records are so packed full of remarkable visions, teasers, strange trails and cliff-hangers that they should all end with the old-fashioned promise 'to be continued'.

So to understand the essence of *Bring 'Em All In*, Mike's new album and his first solo work, you have to return to July 1993, to a sweltering heatwave in Manhattan. Back then, the singer was holding auditions for a new line-up of his band, The Waterboys. The album *Dream Harder* had just been released, and Mike was intending to tour. He'd met up with some gifted rhythm sections and enjoyed a series of great jamming sessions, but still the Scottish-born artist felt something was lacking.

'I realised I wasn't finding a band,' Mike recalls. 'And that fact spoke loud and clear to me. I began to think that maybe I'm not to have a band right now. Maybe I'm supposed to go out on my own for a while.' Effectively, this was the end of The Waterboys and their unique 12-year history. The group had been a commercial success, with three Top five albums in the U.K. Mike had gained artistic recognition in 1992 when his hit song 'The Whole Of The Moon' won an Ivor Novello Award. But more importantly to the many thousands of fans, The Waterboys had bene of huge emotional value – a group that truly meant something.

He relocated to Scotland, staying for a while at the famous Findhorn community, which he describes as 'a school, a university of life'. During his time there Mike worked in the kitchens, in the gardens, on himself and on the songs that would eventually crystallise into *Bring 'Em All In*. In fact, it was at concerts in the community's theatre that he first performed numbers such as 'Building The City Of Light' and 'What Do You Want Me To Do?'

The new songs were specific and personal, covering issues Mike might only have referred to in an indirect way before, his sources of pain, love and wonder finding full expression.

'I feel that I've always been writing about my life-journey, but it's usually been oblique or shrouded in figurative language – old songs like "This Is The Sea" or "Preparing To Fly" were like that. I just took away the disguise this time, put it in everyday language.' The new style developed during Mike's solo tour which began in September 1994. Relying on just himself, his guitar, a mouth harp and occasional piano, he played over 40 gigs in the following nine months. Mike recorded *Bring 'Em All In* on rented equipment in a small studio in Findhorn. He played all the instruments and co-produced the record with Niko Bolas, known for his work with Neil Young. 'Niko came straight from working with Rod Stewart in Los Angeles,' Mike laughs, 'but he soon got over the culture shock!'

Most of the recordings were first takes, on to which Mike overlaid his guitar and keyboard embellishments. The songs were then mixed twice; in Findhorn and later in New York – though mostly the finished album features the original Findhorn mixes. 'Fresher and truer,' Mike reckons, 'with a warmer feel.'

Mike Scott

Shabba Ranks

It was back home in Jamaica, or 'yard' as the islanders call it, that Shabba began sharpening his lyrical skills. As a child he enjoyed hearing the sound of his own voice echoing through the green, hilly countryside. Years later, his family moved to the Kingston ghetto of Trenchtown, birthplace of the most important figure in the progress of reggae music: Bob Marley. In the city streets, the young man known to his parents as Rexton Rawlston Fernando Gordon found himself surrounded by the vibes of reggae sound systems.

At an early age, he already felt that music might be his calling. 'I used to punch rhythm tracks on a jukebox within a bar and sing along,' Shabba recalls. 'I used to take the ten-cent coins, that is how I started practising. I used to put coins in the jukebox and punch songs by Dennis Brown, Gregory Isaacs, and Leroy Smart.'

At first, Shabba's parents didn't look too kindly on their son's love of music. 'They'd only approve of going to school,' he explains, 'getting an education, being like a pilot or a mechanical engineer.'

Shabba continues, 'I used to call myself "Co-Pilot" because there was a selector from a sound system that I used to chat for and his name was "The Navigator". He spins it on the wheel and I chat it on the mic.' Josey Wales, then one of Shabba's hottest DJs, saw the potential in this youth who had begun calling himself Shabba Ranks. 'Josey Wales started telling me, "You got talent, man. You must take it to the studios." So I lace up my shoes and buckle my belt, and from that day until now, it's not turning back.'

In 1987, Wales introduced Shabba to the legendary Jamaican producer King Jammy. Lightning struck in the studio. The young DJ released a rapid succession of hit tunes that quickly established his name alongside other dancehall Kingpins of the day like Josey Wales and Admiral Bailey. But there were much bigger things ahead.

When Jammy's resident engineer Bobby Digital branched off to form his own label, Shabba began pumping out hit after hit on the Digital B Label. (Many of these tracks were later remixed and reissued on the Epic album *Rough and Ready Vols I & II*.) On the strength of his awesome live performances and recordings for the Jammys and Digital B Labels and for other top JA producers like Gussie Clarke, Steely & Clive, and C. 'Specialist'

Dillon, Shabba secured a groundbreaking major-label deal with Epic Records in 1991.

By this time, Shabba had already made history by bringing the dancehall style to an international audience – even before the gold albums (*As Raw As Ever*, 1991; *X-Tra Naked*, 1992), the Grammy Awards, the world tours and the historic collaborations with KRS-1 ('The Jam'), Maxi Priest ('Housecall'), Johnny Gill ('Slow and Sexy', and Queen latifah ('What 'Cha Gonna Do').

But Shabba maintains his humble philosophy. 'Within the line of music,' he says, 'some of us are prophets. Some of us are poets. Some of us are teachers and some of us are preachers. Shabba just make all music. A welder chooses his welding torch and his welding rod in order to make him a man. I choose the lyrics.'

The lyrics to an old Shabba favourite, 'Respect', come to mind:

Mike and equalizer are the DJ tool
And people come to dance like children going to school
You can't be a mimic, you can't be a fool
You have to present your style and make them know say it rule

Simply Red

Date of Birth:	
Mick Hucknall	**8.6.60**
Star Sign:	**Gemini**

Best Record Positions:

1985	'Money's Too Tight (To Mention)'	No. 13	12 weeks
1986	'Holding Back The Years'	No. 2	13 weeks
1987	'The Right Thing'	No. 11	10 weeks
1987	'Ev'ry Time We Say Goodbye'	No. 11	9 weeks
1989	'It's Only Love'	No. 13	8 weeks
1989	'If You Don't Know Me By Now'	No. 2	10 weeks
1991	'Stars'	No. 8	10 weeks
1992	'For Your Babies'	No. 9	8 weeks

Did You Know . . .?

Simply Red have sold a staggering 23 million albums worldwide and their *Stars* album went 12 times platinum!!! Some record, some voice.

Snap

Snap are unconventional musical trailblazers, which is why they have become one of the most internationally successful German pop acts in history.

With their dance-floor anthem 'The Power', the name Snap became, practically overnight, the worldwide trademark for top-class dance music, strengthened by the succession of hits that followed – 'Oops Up', 'Cult of Snap' and 'Mary Had A Little Boy'.

Snap is a dance act who decided against reproducing their first hit sound many times over just to capitalise on the current trend. Instead they offer a broad-based musical experience with a constant flow of innovative ideas. Their debut album *World Power* went on to become one of dance music's few mega-sellers.

The second album, *The Madman's Return*, produced another No. 1 smash with 'Rhythm Is A Dancer', a No. 2 with 'Exterminate' and No. 10 with 'Do You See The Light', and went on to sell over 350,000 in the U.K. alone.

Snap

With *Welcome To Tomorrow* the story continues. The first single, the title track, reached No. 6 here and the second, 'The First The Last Eternity', reached No. 15. Who or what Snap really are seem to be a secret for the chosen few! Snap themselves, whether consciously or not, have helped fan the mystery. It began with the many pseudonyms used by the two Frankfurt-based producers and composers, Michael Muenzing and Luca Anzilotti. As DJs they were only too aware of the preconceived notions about German productions and decided to list themselves in the credits of Snap's first album as Benito Benites and John 'Virgo' Garrett III. The mystery continued with the comings and goings of the singers who occupied the stage with the rapper Turbo B: Jackie Harris, Penny Ford and Thea Austin, Niki Haris – and now Paula Brown, alias Summer.

For the record the voices are . . .

Turbo B: Real name Durron Maurice Butler. He was sent to Frankfurt in 1985 by his Uncle Sam. Rick Sparc discovered he was a first-class rapper and human beat-box. Hit talents earned him spots with acts such as Maze and The Fat Boys.

Jackie Harris: Turbo met her at the concert when she was working for Moses P.

Penny Ford: Has sung for Chaka Khan, Kool and The Gang, George Clinton and The SOS Band.

Thea Austin: Started out performing in bars and clubs in LA and was a friend of Penny Ford who introduced her to Michael and Luca when she left the band.

Niki Haris: Had sung with Madonna for seven years before replacing Thea – she was also introduced to Michael and Luca via Penny Ford.

Summer: Born in Washington DC, this Snap singer met the Snap boys via both Niki and Penny. She has danced with Prince and Janet Jackson and sung with Paula and Snoop Doggy Dog.

Snap may just have played their cards right!

Jimmy Somerville

Glaswegian Jimmy Somerville first shot to fame back in 1984 with groundbreaking band Bronski Beat's 'Smalltown Boy'. Their debut single, it made the Top 3 in Britain and was a huge hit all over Europe. It not only introduced the world to Jimmy's unusual 'falsetto squeal', as he once described it, but confronted them with a lyric addressing the isolation and rejection felt by a provincial gay youth forced into leaving town.

Although not the first pop song to deal with this topic, the chart-friendly early 80s electronic dance sound and the everyday ordinariness and honesty made 'Smalltown Boy' the biggest obviously gay record there'd ever been.

Bronski Beat went on to have several lively pop dance hits in 1984 and 1985 including a cover of former gay icon Donna Summer's 'I Feel Love', on which they joined forces with Marc Almond.

A year of hit records across Europe and the U.K., live performances, outspoken interviews and the pressure of new found fame took their toll. Something of a reluctant star, Jimmy left Bronski Beat for a rest. In a matter of months, however, he was back, forming The Communards with old friend and keyboardist Richard Coles. Over the next three years The Communards enjoyed a string of hits from their two big-selling albums Communards (1986) and Red (1987).

Jimmy and Richard's material was a mixture of good old-fashioned 'gay' disco and more bluesy, acoustic, political and social comment songs, both of which made a strong impact in the Thatcherite 80s and perfectly reflected the two sides of Jimmy's personality. One moment The Communards were hurtling to the No. 1 spot, a position they held for four weeks in September 1986, with an energetic, hedonistic cover version of the Philly Soul classic 'Don't Leave Me This Way'; the next they were stunning audiences into silent awe with their touching lament for a loved one lost to Aids, 'For A Friend'.

At the end of 1988, Richard, a former church organist, left to pursue a career in the media as a religious commentator. Jimmy then embarked on a solo career which saw him chalk up another five hit singles and two albums, Read My Lips (1989) and The Singles Collection (1990). These included another stirring disco cover, of Sylvester's 'You Make Me Feel (Mighty Real)' which made the Top 5, and Françoise Hardy's 'Comment Te Dire Adieu', a duet in French with Jules Miles Kingston. He also contributed to the Aids awareness project album Red Hot And Blue, recording a cover of Cole Porter's 'From The Moment On'.

Jimmy's continued outspokenness on gay issues didn't prevent his records being played and selling in huge quantities. His honesty as a gay performer almost certainly helped pave the way.

Since he disappeared from the charts in 1991, Jimmy has deliberately taken time out from his high profile celebrity existence to, as he put it, live his life to the full as a gay man in the 90s. His new solo material will draw, if anything even more than before, on his personal experiences and the periods of both elation and anger he has passed through in the last three years. Although he has dabbled in some film work, appearing in Sally Potter's Orlando and setting up a gay film company, Normal Films, with Isaac Julien and others to produce Postcards From America, which previewed at 1994's New York Film Festival, the singing voice has taken a long holiday.

'In the last few years,' says Jimmy, 'I've really lived life and discovered myself. I've also discovered what it's like to be part of a peer group that's been touched by the grief and anger of Aids, which has taken away several close friends. The new songs I've written deal with these very personal experiences of life, love, sex and death.'

The album *Dare To Love* was released in June 1995 and is a typical roller-coaster mix of upbeat pop dance numbers and more serious songs exploring gay issues. The first single released from *Dare To Love* was 'Heartbeat' released on January 16 1995. It entered the U.K. charts at No. 24 and was No. 1 in the U.S.A. dance chart. The E-Smoove and the Armand Van Heldon mixes are still being played in clubs today. This was followed by the fabulous cover version of Susan Cadogan's 1975 Top 4 reggae hit 'Hurts So Good'.

'It seemed such a great song to do,' says Jimmy. 'It's about putting up with anything, about being brave in the face of emotional and physical abuse and bouncing back.'

'Hurts So Good' stormed into the U.K. charts at No. 15 and was followed by an outstanding *Top Of The Pops* performance. It was Europe's fourth most played record for four weeks.

Jimmy Somerville is a small-town boy with an up-town talent.

Lisa Stansfield

Lisa's musical career started in Rochdale in 1986 when she formed the band Blue Zone with schoolmates Andy Morris and Ian Devaney. Three years on, a collaboration with Coldcut led to Lisa guesting on their 'People Hold On' track. The combination proved to be inspired. The single climbed the British Top 10 and has since become a club classic. Work then commenced on her debut solo album with Ian and Andy. The first release, 'This Is The Right Time', reached No. 13 in the British chart, with the follow-up, 'All Around The World', hitting No. 1 throughout the U.K. and Europe.

The album, *Affection*, entered the British chart at No. 2 and remained in the U.K. Top 30 for six months after its release. *Affection* eventually reached triple platinum status in the U.K. and sold over four million copies worldwide.

Lisa had no formal voice training to guide her. Her musical inspiration comes from soul music and Motown. In 1990, she achieved a first in musical history, topping the *Billboard* Black Music Chart with

'All Around The World' and 'You Can't Deny It', making her the only British female singer to achieve two consecutive No. 1s in a chart traditionally dominated by American artists.

In November 1990, Lisa recorded a version of Cole Porter's 'Down In The Depths' for the *Red Hot and Blue* LP which helped raise funds for Aids Research Worldwide. Her first tour took place in the spring and summer of 1990, starting in the U.K. and continuing throughout America and Europe, followed by live performances in 1991 at Rock In Rio, The Simple Truth Concert and Red Hot & Dance.

In addition to hit records in Europe and America, Lisa's considerable talents as a singer/songwriter have been recognised by numerous awards. She received two Brit Awards (Best Newcomer, 1989-90 and Best Female Artist, 1990-91), two Ivor Novello Awards in consecutive years for 'All Around The World' (Best Contemporary Song, 1990 and Best International Song, 1991) and a much-coveted Silver Clef Award (Best New Artist, 1990). In America she was nominated for two Grammy Awards in 1991, received the US *Billboard* Award for Best Newcomer 1990, and was voted the Best New Female Singer by readers of *Rolling Stone* magazine. What a launchpad!

The international success of her music, both in terms of critical acclaim and volume of sales, has not changed her one bit. Lisa remains based in Rochdale and has even set up her own recording studio near her home. As Lisa comments, 'I've no desire to move from Rochdale. When I'm not touring I want to be near my friends and family.'

Lisa Stansfield has her feet firmly planted on the ground whilst her musical talent orbits the globe.

Date of Birth:

Peter Kircher	21.1.48
Alan Lancaster	7.2.49
Andy Brown	27.3.49
Francis Rossi	29.5.49
Roy Lynnes	25.11.43

Star Sign:

Peter	Aquarius
Alan	Aquarius
Andy	Aries
Francis	Gemini
Roy	
Sagittarius	

Best Record Positions:

1974	'Down Down'	No. 1	11 weeks
1986	'In The Army Now'	No. 2	14 weeks
1990	'Anniversary Waltz'	No. 2	9 weeks

Supergrass

Supergrass have been in this business for years. But
that doesn't mean they're jaded or they've seen or
done it all. It just means they started early. Very
early. When drummer Danny Goffey was but ten years
old (back in 1985) he had already tasted stardom in
the semi-mythical, pre-pubescent Fallopian Tubes
whose infamous 'My Wife Shut My Gonads In The
Door' elevated him to a position where he could 'sign
autographs in return for a peek at girls' knickers'.
Later, but not much later, inspired by the success of
fellow Oxfordians Ride, he and singer Gaz Coombes
(one year his junior) formed The Jennifers at Wheatley
Comprehensive. With the whole band still ineligible to
vote, The Jennifers released one single for Nude
Records, 'Just Got Back Today' (now a collectors
item), but as shoegazing collapsed around them, the
band dissolved. With Danny and Gaz vowing to work
together again and immersing themselves in Jimi
Hendrix, The Beatles and The Beach Boys, Danny,
implausibly, found work as a dinner lady whilst Gaz
took a job at his local Harvester where he befriended
Brighton Poly graduate Mick Quinn. The trio gelled
into Theodore Supergrass, later shortened to the
vastly superior Supergrass.

For months, the 'Grass honed their craft in various
Oxford clubs before local label Backbeat put out the
Single 'Caught By The Fuzz', a sorry tale of youthful
indiscretions and their aftermath, which leapt into the
Top 65 of John Peel's Festive 50. The buzz was
immediate and, following a tip-off from Radiohead's
management, Parlophone stole a march on the
competition and signed the band.

Things started to escalate. The band supported Blur
and Ride at the Alexandra Palace and the Royal
Albert Hall respectively. Parlophone re-released
'Caught By The Fuzz' which entered the UK Top 50 in
October 1994. Four months later, 'Mansize Rooster',
reached No. 20. The third 'Lenny', climbed to No. 10.
The fourth, 'Alright' was statistically at No. 2 but a
spiritual No. 1 and was heard ringing cheeringly from
every transistor radio, ghetto blaster and pub jukebox
over the long hot summer of 1995. Meantime, cool
US label Sub-Pop imported yellow-vinyl 7" copies of
'Lost It' into the UK – the single shot straight to No.
1 in the UK indie chart.

When Supergrass' debut album 'I Should Coco' was
released, sober broadsheet types and inkie scribblers
fell over themselves to praise the group to the skies.
Unusually, the hyperbole was completely justified in

this case – 'I Should Coco' being one of the most robust, energising British debuts in years. It had all the things we have come to love about the group – top tunes and irrepressible cheek – plus a few hints towards previously unimagined musical maturity. Fittingly, it reached No. 1 in the UK album chart. There followed an idyllic late summer for the band of major European festivals, including the NME stage at the Glastonbury Festival and an unforgettable performance in a steaming marquee at Glasgow's T In The Park weekend.

Following their nomination for the 1995 Mercury Music Prize, the band won two awards at the NME Brat Awards (Best Newcomer and Radio One Session Of The Year). Supergrass were nominated for three Brit Awards, and walked away with Best Newcomer. No. 1 debut album 'I Should Coco' achieved platinum status (selling over 400,000 copies) and the band are currently working on their second album (in Oxford) for release late 1996.

A new single 'Going Out', their first with a horn section and evidence of their ever-growing confidence, was released in February 1996.

How did they get there so quickly? Some of it is attitude . . . and whereas that normally means being a dim ingrate, with Supergrass it means being roguishly charming and very British. Partly, it's their striking visual style that has led young admirers to affect adhesive sideburns and attracted salivating fashion editors worldwide. But mostly it's about music. Great music that's a heady, boisterous meshing of three decades of British pop culture; the casual hedonism of the 60s, the spleen and energy of punk and an eclectic knowingness that is pure 90s.

Supergrass

Take That

In 1991 pop music was getting a bit on the boring side. The charts needed an exciting new group and little did they know there was one lurking just around the corner!

No one took much notice when a song called 'Do What U Like' was released that year as it limped into the charts at No. 82 and limped back out again. But five young guys – Jason Orange, Gary Barlow, Mark Owen, Howard Donald, Robbie Williams and their manager Nigel weren't going to be defeated by one flop.

Take That were determined to make it big and they took heart when their next single 'Promises' reached No. 38 in the charts. Things were looking up.

They immediately released 'Once You've Tasted Love' and 'It Only Takes A Minute', a cover version of an old 60s song by soul supremos The Tavares. It was the first song the group had released that Gaz hadn't written and they felt it was make or break time. It peaked at No. 7 in the charts. Take That were on their way!

They followed up this Top 10 success with 'I Found Heaven' which became a Top 20 hit and consolidated their progress, but this was not good enough for the boys. They decided it was time to take a risk! 'We've always tended to go against the grain and do what people least expect us to do. It keeps us on our toes,' says Gaz.

Certainly no one expected a dancy pop group to jeopardise everything by releasing a slushy ballad. Even their record company RCA had a fit at the very thought. But when 'A Million Love Songs' (a song Gaz had written when he was just 15!) reached No. 7 in the charts, practically the entire country fell in love with the five lads from Manchester.

'That was when things really started happening for us and we just couldn't believe it,' recalls Mark. 'We started to meet other famous people and we were so star-struck it was embarrassing!'

Before they knew it their album *Take That and Party* had shot to No. 2; the No. 1 video *Take That and Party* is still the biggest-selling music video of all time!

But it wasn't enough to sell records. It was time to do something big – a tour.

At 3.00am on a cold windy night in Newcastle the group's coach arrived at the hotel. Inside were five exhausted, nervous lads and they couldn't wait to get on stage.

They were worried. Would the venues sell out? Would their fans like the show? Would they get good reviews? Would anyone really care the group were going on tour? Would there be any fans at the hotel? Their worries were completely unfounded. The tour was mental!

This was to be only the first of many brilliant tours. Meanwhile there were more hits: 'Could It Be Magic' was the Christmas 1992 No. 3 and Take That won a record seven *Smash Hits* Awards. Only the year before they had been watching the show on TV upset that they hadn't been asked to go on. Now here they were just one year on – breaking all records!

1993 was pure magic. 'Pray' reached the coveted No. 1 position, which was followed to the top by 'Relight My Fire'. And not everything changed in the album charts as their *Everything Changes* perched proudly at No. 1. That was not the end of their chart success either as 'Babe' became their third consecutive No. 1 single, making Take That the only group in history to have had three No. 1 records one after the other. They then went on to beat their own record when 'Everything Changes' again went to No. 1 in the spring of 1994.

1994 was one hell of a year in Take Thatsville. The European leg of the Everything Changes tour almost finished them off, with ten sell-out gigs in Germany and arenas bursting at the seams in Denmark, Finland and Sweden.

'We knew we had started to sell records in Europe,' says Mark. 'But doing a tour is another thing. We had no real idea of how well the tickets would sell. When we arrived and found out we had sold out everywhere, we were amazed.' They did one corking show after another, ate a million dodgy curries, all got colds and came home exhausted.

In April Gary got his Ivor Novello Awards – he took his mum to the bash (ah!) and Howard watched the whole thing on TV. 'I remember turning on Sky News and there was Gary and Elton John. I couldn't see his mum though. He must have told her not to steal the limelight!'

While 'Love Ain't Here Anymore' was racing up the charts to the No. 3 slot in July their saucy *Everything Changes* long-form video went to No. 1. There followed the Pops Tour and their single 'Sure', and Howard showed his bum off to boot! 'Sure' went straight in at No. 1 and the entire world wrote sonnets about Howard's rear end!

1995 saw the launch of the group's own magazine 'Take That Official' and in February they sang their single 'Back For Good' at the Brit Awards. On release in March it went straight in at No. 1 and stayed there for four weeks. Their album *Nobody Else* hit the record shops in May and again made top of the charts!

Just as their next single 'Never Forget' was about to be released, Robbie decided to go his own way and signed a highly lucrative recording deal with Richard Branson's Virgin Records.

Meanwhile, Take That go from strength to strength. You can do and say what you like, but the fab four's answer is clearly . . . take that!

Stop Press

News that Take That are breaking up has just been announced, breaking many a girl's heart. But Take That have decided to quit while they're ahead and go their separate ways, so that's that.

Take That

Date of Birth:

Gary Barlow	20.1.71
Howard Donald	27.4.70
Jason Orange	10.7.70
Robbie Williams	13.2.74
Mark Owens	27.1.74

Star Sign:

Gary	Capricorn
Howard	Taurus
Jason	Cancer
Robbie	Aquarius
Mark	Aquarius

Best Record Positions:

1992	'A Million Love Songs'	No. 7	9 weeks
1992	'Could It Be Magic'	No. 3	12 weeks
1993	'Why Can't I Wake Up With You'	No. 2	10 weeks
1993	'Pray'	No. 1	11 weeks
1993	'Relight My Fire'	No. 1	14 weeks
1993	'Babe'	No. 1	10 weeks
1994	'Everything Changes'	No. 1	10 weeks
1994	'Love Ain't Here Anymore'	No. 3	10 weeks
1994	'Sure'	No. 1	12 weeks

Therapy?

Andy Cairns (vocal/guitar), Michael McKeegan (bass/vocals) and Fyfe Ewing (drums/vocals) came together, as a result of a common interest in the theories of 'noise, chaos and mass anxiety'. Whatever reasoning drew them in, Therapy? had managed to ink a deal and release their debut album for the influential Wiiija label by the summer of 1991. The aptly titled *Baby Teeth* displayed early signs of songwriting ingenuity with the frantic 'Skyward' and the beguiling 'Dancin' With Manson'. It was followed at the beginning of 1992 by the fiercely mature mini-album *Pleasure Death*, featuring the now infamous 'Potato Junkie'.

Therapy? crowned their achievements late in the year by making the jump to A&M to record *Nurse*. From the technical overload of 'Teethgrinder', to the melodic bite of 'Nausea', *Nurse* gave the band a Top 30 album and announced their arrival in style. With success breeding success and the band's live show rapidly becoming an event in itself, three distinctive EPs – 'Shortsharpshock' (featuring the classic 'Screamager'), 'Face The Strange' and 'Opal Mantra' - brought the band *Top Of The Pops* appearances, sell-out shows and led them seamlessly into the release of *Troublegum* in 1994. This album not only exceeded the expectations of those anticipating great things for the band, it also pleasantly surprised those who had dismissed the Larne trio as simply a post-modern Undertones or a lightened-up Big Black. *Troublegum* was a *tour de force*, a melodic, angst-fuelled joyride through songwriter Andy Cairns' darkest demons. As massive chart success throughout Europe bore vivid testimony, smalltown self-loathing had never looked or sounded so good. From the opening lines of 'Knives' – the brilliant 'My girlfriend says that I need help' – through songs like 'Die Laughing', 'Femtex', 'Unbeliever' and the opening single 'Nowhere', *Troublegum* saw the unwritten barriers dividing rock and indie come crashing down.

After a year in which the band notched up over half a million album sales, a Mercury Music prize nomination, and plaudits from the *Daily Telegraph*, a Castle Donnington audience and all points in between, Therapy? began work in 1995 on *Internal Love*. With almost indecent speed – the album was recorded over four weeks with producer Al Clay at Real World Studios in Bath – Therapy? delivered a record that astonishes with its reach, its artfulness and a maturity hitherto only hinted at.

It is the sound of a band really coming of age: instant pop records like the first single 'Stories' or the multi-dimensional 'Loose' rub shoulders easily with epics like 'A Moment Of Clarity' and 'Jude The Obscene'. The album positively abounds with ideas and possibilities. Describing it as an optimistic record may be overstating the case – titles like 'Misery', 'Bad Mother' and 'Bowels Of Love' hardly suggest a record to pull you out of a bad day – but the results are constantly stimulating and always exciting.

Those 2 Girls

Those 2 Girls are Denise Van Outen and Cathy Warwick, both aged 20. They originally met eight years ago at a party but never spoke to each other! The due were re-introduced through their now management/record label boss Denis Ingoldsby, who also looks after Eternal and Dina Carroll.

Denise attended the Sylvia Young Stage School from the age of 11. At 15 she left to star in the TV series *Kappatoo* on ITV. Since then she hasn't stopped working. Last year she co-presented the Carlton teen magazine TV show *The Edge* with model Cassius.

Cathy has just left college after spending three years doing a Performing Arts course at the famous Italia Conti Stage School, during which time she also starred in several TV ads, and toured in the rock 'n' roll musical *Tutti Fruttie*. Cathy was first introduced to Denis by a producer with whom she had previously worked when she had a recording contract with a small independent label. More recently she got to know Denis through her best mate, Louise from Eternal! He thought Cathy had a fantastic voice and it was only a matter of time before they snapped her up to form a new dance/pop band.

Denise met Denis last year at a *Summer* magazine roadshow, where she was appearing with Cassius. They hit it off and have kept in touch ever since. Denis discovered she could sing, and paired Denise up with Cathy forming Those 2 Girls!!

Those 2 Girls was the first act to be signed to the new Final Vinyl label through Arista/BMG Records. Their debut album *Sweet Temptation*, which includes their first hit single 'All I Want', promises that these two girls could well have a party now they have got their act together.

TLC

The acronym TLC took on a new meaning when T-Boz, Left Eye and Chilli made their 1992 debut and refined what R&B and rap listeners could expect from a female act. Salt 'N' Peppa may stand tall in hip-hop circles for their fiercely independent, pro-woman stance, and Mary J. Blige can be hailed as the queen of hip-hop soul, but it is TLC that has successfully combined that comically witty and intuitive lyrical direction and the undeniable groove, swagger and thump of urban life into one persona that is theirs alone.

Their first two hits, 'Ain't 2 Proud 2 Beg' and the mid-tempo ballad 'Baby-Baby-Baby', both became Top 3 platinum singles, and resulted in sales of 2.8 million on their first album *Ooooooohhh . . . On The TLC Tip*. Two years later, TLC returned with *CrazySexyCool* a non-stop, funk-driven ride that kicked the assumption of a sophomore jinx to the curb! *CrazySexyCool* not only described the dominant personality traits of Lisa 'Left Eye' Lopes, Rozonda 'Chilli' Thomas and Tionne 'T-Boz' Watkins, but spoke to all women. '*CrazySexyCool*, to me, is the "I'm Every Woman" of the 90s' explained Chilli. 'Because every woman – I don't care how shy or how outgoing you are or whatever, everybody has got a crazy, sexy, cool side. And depending on the situation and whatever mood you're in, a particular side comes out.'

T-Boz puts it best when she asked, 'Wouldn't y'all like a girl who has a nice sense of humour, that can kick it, make you laugh and then on the other side, in the bedroom, "whip that thang on you?" . . . but when it's time to kick it with the fellas, she can roll and get her stroll on?'

The first single, 'Creep', produced by Dallas Austin (Madonna, Boyz II Men), allowed T-Boz's sensuous, rumbling voice to narrate her escapades outside of a relationship lacking in attention. 'I think that song really worked for them because guys talk about running around on women all day long in songs,' says Austin. 'But girls, it takes a special kind of girl, one that's not always worried about being ladylike and not afraid to speak her mind to do this.'

Soundwise, 'Creep' picked up where the group that ushered in New Jill Swing left off, but visually the girls changed. Gone was the exaggerated look they crafted with cartoonish bright colours and big clothes. And while safe sex is still a priority for TLC, no longer will condoms be pinned all over their clothes. 'I don't want people to think that we contradicted ourselves by coming out saying women can wear whatever they want – pants falling off their butts, hat to the back, whatever – and can still be respected and sexy,' says T-Boz. 'We still think that. And just because we show a little stomach in the video, that's just one side of being *CrazySexyCool*. Our clothes were still baggy and we had completely flipped, coming out wearing dresses and heels.'

'People never know what to expect from TLC as far as

how they're going to look or what they'll do, but when it comes to the music – and this album proves it – you should expect quality!' booms LaFace co-president Antonio Reid proudly. It was his wife, Perri 'Pebbles' Reid, who brought the group to the label's attention.

'TLC is what I call the epitome of entertainment,' she adds. 'They're entertaining on all levels. Whether you're listening to their record, watching them in a movie, watching their videos or just sitting down talking to them and just watching them in a room . . . these girls know how to entertain and their appeal is so broad.'

TLC's talents have burgeoned beyond the confines of the group: they came up with the theme song for Nickelodeon's television show *All That*; co-starred in their first motion picture, *House Party 3*; Left Eye lent her rat-a-tat rhyming skills to Keith Sweat's Top 10 single 'How Do You Like It?'; and all three covered The Time's 'Get It Up' for the *Poetic Justice* soundtrack.

'I look at TLC and I see more than singers, I see characters,' says filmmaker John Singleton, who wrote and directed *Poetic Justice*. 'They're full of energy, personality and creativity, it's only natural they would look beyond working in recording studios.'

UB40

Date of Birth:
Eric Falconer	21.1.59
Micky Vitue	19.1.57
Norman Hassan	26.1.57

Star Sign:
Eric	Aquarius
Micky	Capricorn
Norman	Aquarius

Best Record Positions:
Year	Title	Position	Weeks
1983	'Red Red Wine'	No. 1	14 weeks
1985	'I Got You Babe'	No. 1	13 weeks
1990	'Kingston Town'	No. 4	12 weeks
1993	'(I Can't Help) Falling In Love With You'	No. 1	16 weeks
1993	'Higher Ground'	No. 8	9 weeks

Utah Saints

In the 80s, Jez Willis had been in pioneering and
primal electronic rock band MDMA. Tim Garbutt had
DJ-ed in a myriad of clubs. Where they met, physically
and spiritually, was at Leeds' legendary Mile High
Club – a hothouse of 70s disco and funk hedonism
hosted by the soon-to-be Utahs. And where they met
musically, was in 1991 on a piece of 12#ai plastic
titled *What Can You Do For Me*, which combined a
completely reworked Eurythmics sample with some
furiously hard-edged rhythms and grooves. In one fell
swoop, *What Can You Do For Me* created the Utah
Saints and sent Jez and Tim spinning into the Top 10.
Once the boys had unveiled their distinctive logo,
converse clothing and preposterous 'Pineapple head'
haircuts on *Top Of The Pops*, Utah would no longer be
principally known as a place in the U.S.A. where the
Osmonds came from. Further hits such as 'Something
Good' and 'Believe In Me' (sampling Kate Bush and
The Human League respectively) built on the success
of *What Can You Do For Me*, turning Utah Saints into
a respected and influential dance/rock hybrid and a
commercial sensation.

Although Utah Saints recorded their records as a duo,
for live work they expanded to become a full band –
complete with thumping bass lines and flailing-armed
percussionists. For Jez and Tim, playing live was all
part of the fun of being Utah Saints. It was also very
much a statement, in the same way Jez wearing a

Motorhead T-shirt for their first *Top Of The Pops* appearance was a statement.

'We've always tried to break down categories,' explains Jez. 'So when we play live we try to make it so powerful that it blurs the lines between a rock gig and a dance club.'

If proof were needed, in one week in late 1993, Utah Saints played separate gigs with U2, Take That, East 17, Sister Of Mercy frontman Andrew Eldtritch, and the next night a hardcore Techno rave in Germany! Two years on, live dance music is commonplace and Utah Saints are set to move the goalposts again. Their single 'Ohio' and the *Wired World* album showed that the Utah sound can shift on its axis whilst still being recognisable. Both emerged from Utah Saints' desire to create songs from new sounds, using some very peculiar recording methods. 'We want to make albums that combine a pop sensibility with a full use of the sampler,' enthuses Jez. 'With the sampler there are no limits at all. You can make new sounds or new twists on established ones. There's two ways to make music interesting. One is the way Oasis do it – using a lot of chord changes and stuff – and you've got to be pretty good at it. And personally I think Oasis are good at it. The other is to make it sonically interesting and make new combinations of sounds that you haven't heard before.'

With *Wired World* they sought to make an album that has depth, that would work equally well very loud in a club situation or quietly played at home. They also dreamt of a machine-based record that was moving and that had a lot of emotional energy to it. Utah Saints' creative use of samples is a subject upon which Jez wants to set the record straight. 'We have been criticised for using parts of other people's records,' he claims. 'But we never got credit for the fact that we took incidental parts of those records and made them feature parts of our records. "Something good is gonna happen" is a line from a Kate Bush verse. "What Can You Do For Me" came out of an ad lib at the beginning of the Eurythmics track. "Believe In Me" was the middle rap out of "Love Action". We took incidental bits, made them into choruses and gave them new meaning.'

In the near future Utah Saints promise CD-Rom experiments and the mind-boggling Utahvision – a new form of live performance involving interactive films. That will come later. In the meantime, here's the music.

Whigfield

Whigfield is the stage name of a lovely blonde lady of Danish origin who has decided to make a mark in the history of dance music. Her real name is Sannie Charlotte Carlson, but it's a long time since anyone has called her that.

She left Skaelskar, where she was born, a few years ago to try modelling but she soon realized that her true love was music. She studied music in Denmark, where her teacher made a big impression on her (her name was, in fact, Whigfield). She also sang, from time to time, in her brother's group. Needless to say, her looks and her personality have helped her career. Someone told Larry Pignagnoli (who was already famous for launching Spagna on their way to international success) about Whigfield and he immediately saw that she had what it takes to become a star.

Her first mix, 'Saturday Night', re-released in Italy at the end of 1993, was also a great hit in Spain where it topped the charts for 11 consecutive weeks. From then on, she practically became a household name. In the months that followed, she gave performances in Spain's most famous discos which were an immediate hit. She was then invited to take part in some of Spain's hottest TV shows, such as *Hola! Rafaella*. Due to the success of her second single, 'Another Day', and of the Spanish version of 'Saturday Night' Whigfield toured Italy that summer. Whigfield has a strong temperament, she is 24 years old and born under the sign of Aries. She says that she has a big heart and that she is obsessed by being punctual; she also admits to being a little selfish.

For the record, Whigfield's debut album, *Whigfield*, burst straight into the U.K. album charts at No. 13 in June 1995 and quickly went silver (selling over 60,000 copies). Meanwhile it's also gone gold in Canada and silver in Italy, Germany, Holland and Belgium. The album features her classic No. 2 single 'Saturday Night', her Top 10 follow-up 'Another Day', her next Top 10 single 'Think Of You', her Top 20 single 'Close To You', plus her single 'Big Time'. Whigfield made British music business history by being the first new artist to go straight into the British charts at No. 1 with a debut single! – the single, as if you need to be reminded, was 'Saturday Night'. It sold more copies during its second week of release than any other single since the Band Aid single in 1984 and in the first three weeks of release sold over 750,000 copies in the U.K. alone whilst also being a Top 10 hit all across Europe.

Whigfield's follow-up single, 'Another Day', was a U.K. smash during Christmas 1994, peaking at No. 7 in the charts. Her third single, 'Close To You', also sat pretty at No. 7 in the U.K. charts for two weeks in June 1995, whilst her fourth single, 'Close To You', which spent a month in the U.K. Top 40 and peaked at No. 13, proved Whiggy isn't just a one-hit wonder! Whigfield will be in the 'big time' for a long time to come!

Kim Wilde

Kim Wilde was born into music, her father Marty being one of the 50s biggest chart stars. Tempted into the limelight by her Dad and Ricky (with whom she still collaborates today), her first single, 'Kids In America', took her all the way to No. 2 in the U.K. charts in February 1981. A classic blast of 80s power pop, it set the Wilde wheels in motion, increasing in speed all the time, and now, 14 years later, she's notched up a staggering seven million album sales and 12 million singles, statistics which certify her as one of the most successful British female solo artists of all time.

Now Kim Wilde is back, elegantly striding into the pop arena with *Now and Forever*, her tenth album and the best record she's had her name attached to since, oh, ages.

'*Now and Forever*,' says Kim, is the first album in her entire career which she feels is 100 per cent Kim Wilde. 'Last year, I went out and toured my *Greatest Hits* album and thoroughly enjoyed it, but I also saw it as a major turning point in my career. I started to feel that my musical influences up to that point were wearing a little bit thin, especially after a decade of playing them. So for this album I wanted to spoil myself and record the kind of music I love the most. I'm lucky because I'm in a position where I can make exactly the kind of music I want without any kind of restriction whatsoever.'

Stylistically, *Now and Forever* has its heart deep in soul music, sounding as fresh as a debut with an often frenetic pace and a star-spangled handbag-ful of housey rhythms. From the opening track and first single, 'Breakin' Away', a song so bubbly it positively begs to be described as effervescent, to the turn-the-lights-down-low-then-come-here-and-kiss-me ballads like 'C'Mon Love Me' and 'This I Swear', it's an impressively consistent collection that really does see her turning a brand new leaf. In shedding her former image as the ultimate 80s pop starlet, Kim Wilde has transformed herself into a credible soul diva.

Kim Wilde
Date of Birth: **18.11.60**
Star Sign: **Scorpio**

Best Record Positions:

Year	Title	Position	Weeks
1981	'Kids In America'	No. 2	13 weeks
1986	'You Keep Me Hanging On'	No. 2	14 weeks
1988	'You Came'	No. 3	11 weeks
1992	'Love Is Holy'	No. 16	6 weeks
1993	'If I Can't Have You'	No. 12	8 weeks

At A Glance . . .
Who Do You Share Your Birthday With?

January

1	Grandmaster Flash 1967
2	Harry Travis (Hipsway)1963
3	Melanie 1947
4	Martin McAloon (Prefab Sprout)
5	Biff Byford (Saxon) 1951
6	Syd Barrett (Pink Floyd) 1946
7	Mike McGear (Scaffold) 1944
8	Elvis Presley 1935 David Bowie
9	Scott Walker 1944
10	Pat Benatar 1953
11	Ben Leach (The Farm) 1971
12	Long John Baldry 1941
13	Graham 'Suggs' MacPhearson (Madness) 1961
14	Carl Smith (Madness) 1959
15	Peter Trewavas (Marillion) 1959
16	Sade 1960
17	Jaz Strode (Kaja) 1958
18	Tom Bailey (Thompson Twins) 1957
19	Robert Palmer 1949
20	Tina (Fuzzbox) 1969
21	Peter Kircher (Status Quo) 1948
22	Ray Mayhew (Sigue Sigue Sputnic)
23	Eric Falconer (UB40) 1959
24	Jools Holland (Squeeze) 1958
25	Garry Tibbs (Adam Ant) 1958
26	Andrew Ridgeley (Wham) 1963
27	Gillian Gilbert (New Order) 1961
28	Dave Sharp (Alarm) 1959
29	Roddy Frame (Aztec Camera) 1964
30	Jody Watley 1959
31	Lloyd Cole 1961

February

1	Don Everly 1937
2	Skip Battin (The Byrds) 1934
3	Dave Davis (Kinks) 1947
4	Alice Cooper 1948
5	Jane Eugene (Loose Ends) 1962
6	Rick Astley 1966
7	Carl Hunter (The Farm) 1962
8	Stefan Osadzinski (Roaring Boys) 1960
9	Holly Johnson (FGTH) 1960
10	Clifford T Ward 1946
11	Jill Brysen (Strawberry Switchblade)
12	Mark Fox (Haircut 100) 1959
13	Peter Tork (Monkees) 1945
14	Peter Gabriel 1950
15	Ali Campbell (UB40) 1959
16	Andy Taylor (Duran Duran) 1961
17	Gene Pitney 1941
18	Jasper Stain Thorpe (Then Jerico)
19	Dave Wakeling (General Public) 1956
20	Kee Marcello (Europe) 1960
21	Nina Simone 1933
22	Ranking Roger (General Public) 1963
23	Chris Gentry (Menswear) 1977
24	Paul Jones (Manfred Mann) 1942
25	George Harrison (Beatles) 1943
26	Sandie Shaw 1947
27	Peter Andre 1973
28	Brian Jones (Rolling Stones) 1942
29	Gretchen Christopher (Fleetwood Mac)

Birthdays

March

1   Roger Daltrey (The Who) 1945
2   Jon (Bon Jovi) 1962
3   Mark Rogers (Hollywood Beyond)
4   Shakin' Stevens 1948
5   Andy Gibb (Bee Gees) 1958
6   Dave Gilmour (Pink Floyd) 1944
7   Clive Burr (Iron Maiden) 1957
8   Ralph Ellis (Swinging Blue Jeans) 1942
9   Martin Fry (ABC) 1958
10 Tina Charles 1955
11 Bruce Watson (Big Country) 1961
12 Steve Harris (Iron Maiden) 1957
13 Adam Clayton (U2) 1960
14 Walter Parazaider (Chicago) 1945
15 Terence Trent D'Arby 1960
16 Jimmy Nail 1954
17 Scott Gorham (Thin Lizzy) 1951
18 Wilson Pickett 1941
19 Bruce Willis 1955
20 Richard Drummie (Go West) 1959
21 Slim Jim McDonnell (Stray Cats) 1961
22 Peter Wylie (Wah) 1958
23 David & Michael (Gemini) 1974
24 Nena 1960
25 Elton John 1947
26 Diana Ross 1944
27 Andy Brown (Status Quo) 1947
28 Cheryl James (Salt 'N' Peppa) 1969
29 Mick Roberts (King) 1962
30 Eric Clapton 1945
31 Angus Young (AC/DC) 1959

April

1	Stuart Black (Menswear) 1975
2	Karen Woodward (Bananarama) 1961
3	Barry Pritchard (The Fortunes) 1944
4	Dave Hill (Slade) 1952
5	Agnetha Faltskog (Abba) 1950
6	Colin Ferguson (H2O) 1961
7	Simon Climie (Climie Fisher) 1960
8	Julian Lennon 1963
9	Mark Kelly (Marillion) 1961
10	Katrina Leskanish (Katrina And The Waves)
11	Neville Staples (Fun Boy Three)
12	David Cassidy 1950
13	Jim Pons (Turtles) 1946
14	Patrick Fairley (Marmalade) 1946
15	Sam Fox 1966
16	Nick Berry 1963
17	Stephen Singleton (ABC) 1959
18	Shirlie Holliman (Pepsi & Shirlie)
19	Alan Price (Animals) 1942
20	Luther Vandross 1951
21	Robert Smith (The Cure) 1959
22	Peter Frampton (1950
23	Roy Orbison 1936
24	Captain Sensible 1955
25	Fish (Marillion) 1958
26	Roger Taylor (Duran Duran)
27	Sheena Easton 1959
28	Glenn Miller Records Pennsylvania 65000
29	Lonnie Donegan 1931
30	Merrill Osmond 1953

Birthdays

May

1   Ray Parker Jnr 1954
2   Dr Robert (Blow Monkeys) 1961
3   Peter Staples (Troggs) 1944
4   Jackie Jackson 1951
5   Bill Ward (Black Sabbath) 1945
6   Larry Steinbachek (Bronski Beat)
7   Rick Westwood (Tremeloes) 1943
8   Gary Glitter 1940
9   Billy Joel 1949
10   Bono 1960
11   Eric Burdon (Animals) 1941
12   Billy Duffy (The Cult) 1961
13   Stevie Wonder 1950
14   David Byrne (Talking Heads) 1962
15   Graham Clark (Wet Wet Wet) 1966
16   Janet Jackson 1966
17   Alan Bankine (Associates) 1958
18   Toyah 1958
19   Martin Ware (Heaven 17) 1956
20   Nick Heyward 1961
21   Timothy Lever (Dead Or Alive) 1961
22   Morrissey 1959
23   Theresa Dorar 1957
24   Helen Terry 1956
25   Paul Weller (Style Council) 1958
26   Wayne Hussey (The Mission) 1959
27   Siouxsie (Siouxsie And The Banshees) 1957
28   Kylie Minogue 1968
29   Mel Gaynor (Simple Minds) 1960
30   Stephen Duffy 1960
31   Wendy Smith (Prefab Sprout) 1963

June

1	Ronnie Wood (Rolling Stones) 1947	
2	Charlie Watts (Rolling Stones) 1941	
3	Suzi Quatro 1950	
4	Gordon Waller (Peter and Gordon)	
5	Mags (Fuzzbox) 1964	
6	D C Lee 1961	
7	Prince 1958	
8	Mick Hucknall (Simply Red) 1960	
9	Eddie Lundon (China Crisis) 1962	
10	Mark Shaw (Then Jerico) 1961	
11	Lynsey De Paul 1950	
12	Reg Presley (Troggs) No Date	
13	Denise Pearson (5 Star) 1968	
14	Boy George 1961	
15	Noddy Holder (Slade) 1950	
16	Errol Kennedy (Imagination) 1953	
17	Barry Manilow 1946	
18	Paul McCartney (Beatles) 1942	
19	Mark Debarge (Debarge) 1959	
20	John Taylor (Duran Duran) 1960	
21	Marky Mark 1971	
22	Tony Cunningham (Wet Wet Wet)	
23	Marti Pellow (Wet Wet Wet) 1966	
24	Curt Smith (Tears For Fear) 1961	
25	George Michael 1963	
26	Tony Hadley (Spandau Ballet) 1960	
27	Steve Price (Hurrah) 1965	
28	Dave Knights (Procol Harum) 1945	
29	Colin Hay (Men At Work) 1953	
30	Andy Scott (Sweet) 1951	

Birthdays

July

1	Simon White (Menswear) 1974
2	Pete Briquette (Boomtown Rats)
3	Vince Clarke (Erasure) 1961
4	DJ David 'Kid' Jensen 1950
5	Huey Lewis 1950
6	John Keeble (Spandau Ballet) 1959
7	Ringo Starr (Beatles) 1940
8	Andy Fletcher (Depeche Mode) 1961
9	Jim Kerr (Simple Minds) 1959
10	Neil Tennant (Pet Shop Boys) 1954
11	Pete Murphy (Bauhaus) 1957
12	Gary Tarn (Drum Theatre) 1962
13	Roger McQuinn (Byrds) 1942
14	Chris Cross (Ultravox) 1952
15	Linda Ronstadt 1946
16	Stewart Copeland (Police) 1952
17	Mick Tucker (Sweet) 1943
18	Nigel Twist (The Alarm) 1958
19	Brian May (Queen) 1950
20	Michael McNeil (Simple Minds) 1958
21	Cat Stephens 1947
22	Pat Badger (Extreme) 1967
23	David Essex 1947
24	Alan Whitehead (Marmalade) 1945
25	Jim McCarty (Yardbirds) 1943
26	Mick Jagger (Rolling Stones) 1943
27	Paul Court (Primitives) 1965
28	Steve Took (T Rex) 1949
29	John Sykes (Whitesnake) 1959
30	Kate Bush 1958
31	Malcolm Ross (Orange Juice) 1960

August

1	Joe Elliot (Def Leppard) 1960
2	Pete De Freitas (Echo And The Bunnymen) 1961
3	Kirk Brandon (Spear Of Destiny)
4	Paul Reynolds (Flock Of Seagulls)
5	Pete Burns (Dead Or Alive) 1959
6	Mike Nocito (Johnny Hates Jazz)
7	Ian Dench (EMF) 1967
8	Dave 'The Edge' Evans (U2) 1961
9	Whitney Houston 1964
10	Ian Anderson (Jethro Tull) 1947
11	Paul Gendler (Modern Romance)
12	Mark Knopfler (Dire Straits) 1949
13	Ian Haughland (Europe) 1964
14	David Crosby (Crosby, Stills & Nash)
15	Mikey Graham 1972
16	Madonna 1958
17	Kevin Rowland (Dexys) 1952
18	John Rees (Men At Work) 1957
19	Joey Tempest (Europe) 1963
20	Robert Plant 1948
21	Glenn Hughes (Deep Purple) 1952
22	Roland Orzabal (Tears For Fears)
23	Bobby Gee (Bucks Fizz) 1954
24	Jeffrey Daniel (Shalamar) 1958
25	Elvis Costello 1954
26	Danny White (Matt Bianco) 1959
27	Glen Matlock (Sex Pistols) 1955
28	Dan Seraphine (Chicago) 1948
29	Michael Jackson 1958
30	Mick Moody (Whitesnake) 1950
31	Debbie Gibson 1970

Birthdays

September

1   Gloria Estefan 1958
2   Nicholas Ashford (Ashford And Simpson) 1943
3   Al Jardine (Beach Boys) 1942
4   Martin Chambers (Pretenders) 1951
5   David Clempson (Humble Pie)
6   Buster Bloodvessel (Bad Manners)
7   Chrissie Hynde 1951
8   David Steele (Fine Young Cannibals)
9   Dave Stewart (Eurythmics) 1952
10   Don Powell (Slade) 1948
11   Jon Moss (Culture Club) 1957
12   Neil Peart (Rush) 1952
13   Matt Everett (Menswear) 1972
14   Morten Harket (A-Ha) 1959
15   Jaki Graham 1956
16   Joe Butler (Lovin' Spoonful) 1943
17   Lol Creme (Godley And Creme) 1947
18   Joanne Catherhall (Human League)
19   Rusty Egan (Visage) 1957
20   Allanah Currie (Thompson Twins)
21   Don Felder (Eagles) 1947
22   Joan Jett 1958
23   Bruce Springsteen 1949
24   Gerry Marsden (Gerry And The Pacemakers) 1942
25   Declan Donnelly (PJ And Duncan)
26   Tracy Thorn (Everything But The Girl)
27   Meatloaf 1951
28   Paul Handyside (Hurrah) 1960
29   Matt And Luke Goss (Bros) 1968
30   Basia (Matt Bianco) 1954

October

1   Rob Danes (Mud) 1947
2   Sting 1951
3   Lindsey Buckingham (Fleetwood Mac) 1947
4   Peter Hooton (The Farm) 1966
5   Bob Geldof 1954
6   Richard Jobson (The Armoury Show)
7   Martin Murray (Honeycombes) 1941
8   Robert 'Kool' Bell (Kool And The Gang)
9   John Lennon 1940
10 Midge Ure 1953
11 Luke Perry 1965
12 Rick Parfitt (Status Quo) 1948
13 Paul Simon (1941
14 Cliff Richard 1940
15 Tito Jackson 1953
16 Gary Kemp (Spandau Ballet) 1959
17 Bernadette Nolan 1961
18 Tim May (Roaring Boys) 1960
19 Sinitta 1966
20 Mark King (Level 42) 1958
21 Tony Mortimer (East 17) 1970
22 Eddie Brigati (Rascals) 1946
23 Michael Mertens (Propaganda) 1963
24 Bill Wyman (Rolling Stones) 1936
25 John Leven (Europe) 1963
26 Steve Wren (Then Jerico) 1962
27 Simon Le Bon (Duran Duran) 1958
28 Hank Marvin (Shadows) 1941
29 Jerry Lee Lewis 1935
30 Otis Miles (Temptations) 1941
31 Vanilla Ice 1968

November

1	Mags Furuholmen (A-Ha) 1961
2	Chips Hawkes (Tremeloes) 1945
3	Marilyn 1962
4	Chris Difford (Squeeze) 1954
5	Peter Noone (Hermans Hermits)
6	Ethan Hawke 1971
7	Joni Mitchell 1943
8	Terry Harron (Adam And The Ants)
9	Sandy Denton (Salt 'N' Peppa) 1969
10	Neil Weir (OMD) 1961
11	Ian Craigmarsh (Heaven 17) 1956
12	Les McKeown (Bay City Rollers) 1955
13	Terry Reid 1949
14	Freddie Garrity (Freddie And The Dreamers)
15	Tony Thompson (Power Station)
16	Gene Clark (Byrds) 1941
17	Pete Cox (Go West) 1955
18	Kim Wilde 1960
19	Bill Sharp (Shakatak) 1952
20	Michael Diamond (Beastie Boys)
21	Alex James (Blur) 1968
22	Tina Weymouth (Talking Heads) 1950
23	Sandra Stevens (Brotherhood Of Man)
24	John Squire (Stone Roses) 1962
25	Steve Rothesay (Marillion) 1959
26	Tina Turner 1939
27	Charles Burchill (Simple Minds)
28	David Van Day 1957
29	Ryan Giggs 1973
30	Billy Idol 1955

December

1   Gilbert O'Sullivan 1946

2   Rick Savage (Def Leppard) 1960

3   Ozzy Osbourne 1948

4   Chris Hillman (Byrds) 1942

5   Les Nemes (Haircut 100) 1960

6   Ben Watt (Everything But The Girl)

7   Mike Nolan (Bucks Fizz) 1954

8   Sinead O'Connor 1966

9   Joan Armatrading 1950

10   Frank Beard (ZZ Top) 1951

11   David Gates (Bread) 1940

12   John Dean (Menswear) 1971

13   Dave O'List (Nice) 1950

14   Mike Scott (Waterboys) 1958

15   Dave Clark 1942

16   Tony Hicks (Hollies) 1943

17   Sarah Dallin (Bananarama) 1961

18   Keith Richards (Rolling Stones)

19   Limahl 1958

20   Peter Criss (Kiss) 1942

21   Carl Wilson (Beach Boys) 1946

22   Maurice And Robin Gibb (Bee Gees)

23   Dave Murray (Iron Maiden) 1958

24   Lemmy (Motorhead) 1945

25   Annie Lennox (Eurythmics) 1956

26   Abdul Fakir (Four Tops) 1935

27   Mike Pender (Moody Blues) 1942

28   Chas Hodges (Chas And Dave) 1943

29   Cozy Powell 1947

30   Jeff Lynne (ELO) 1947

31   Scott Ian (Anthrax) 1963